THE BEST OF
EASY KNITS
for boys and girls

BayBooks
An imprint of HarperCollins*Publishers*

A BAY BOOKS PUBLICATION
An imprint of HarperCollinsPublishers

First published in Australia in 1991 by Bay Books, of
CollinsAngus&Robertson Publishers Pty Limited (ACN 009 913 517)
A division of HarperCollinsPublishers (Australia) Pty Limited
25–31 Ryde Road, Pymble NSW 2073, Australia

HarperCollinsPublishers (New Zealand) Limited
31 View Road, Glenfield, Auckland 10, New Zealand

HarperCollinsPublishers Limited
77– 85 Fulham Palace Road, London W6 8JB, United Kingdom

National Library of Australia
Cataloguing-in-Publication data:

   [Easy knits for boys and girls]. Best of easy knits
   for boys and girls.

   ISBN 1 86378 002 5.

   1. Knitting — Patterns. 2. Children's clothing — Patterns.
   I. Title: Easy knits for boys and girls.

746.92

Typeset in Helvetica Light
Printed in Singapore

5 4 3 2 1
95 94 93 92

CONTENTS

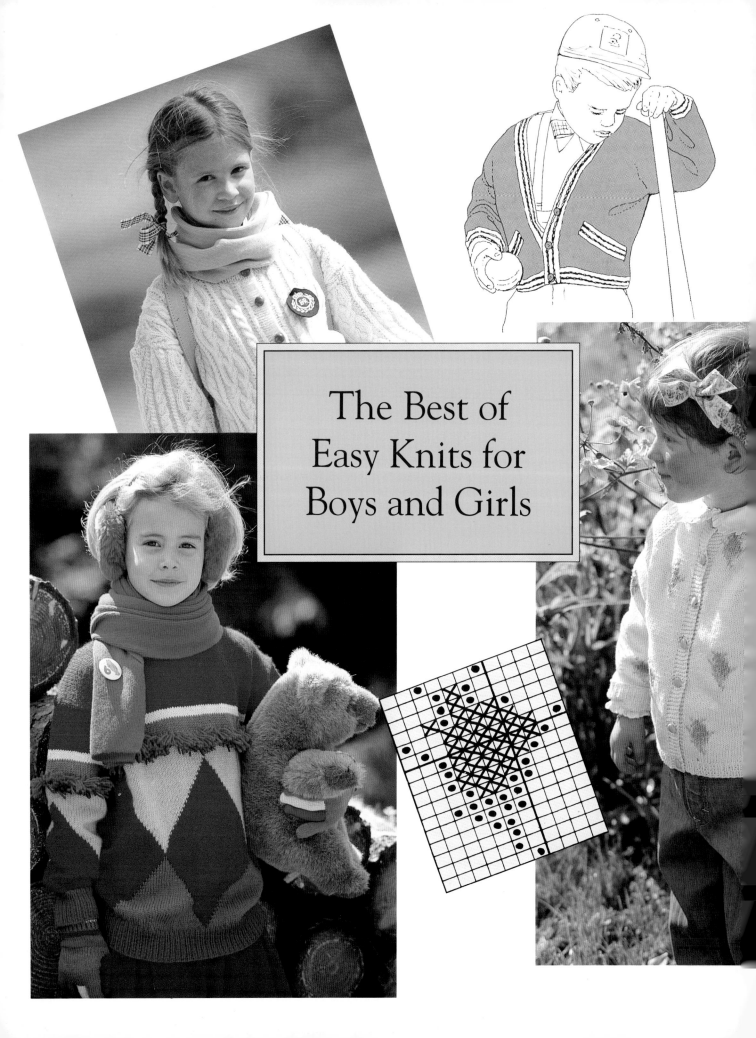

The Best of Easy Knits for Boys and Girls

BEST OF EASY KNITS FOR BOYS AND GIRLS is a treasure trove of patterns for children from tiny tots to pre-teens, for summer and winter or in-between. There are styles to suit a beginner and styles to challenge the expert. This is the fourth book in our EASY KNITS series and is certain to become a favourite you will use again and again.

Abbreviations

alt = alternate; **amt** = amount; **beg** = beginning; **comm** = commencing; **cont** = continue; **dec** = decrease; **fin** = finished; **foll** = following; **g st** = garter stitch; **inc** = increase; **incl** = including; **k** = knit; **k2 tog** = knit 2 together; **lhs** = left hand side; **meas** = measures; **0** = (zero) — no stitches, times or rows; **p** = purl; **patt** = pattern; **psso** = pass slip stitch over; **rem** = remaining; **rep** = repeat; **rhs** = right hand side; **rsf** = right side facing; **rsr** = right side row; **sl** = slip; **sl st** = slip stitch; **sl 2 tog** = slip 2 together; **st(s)** = stitch(es); **st st** = stocking stitch; **wsf** = wrong side facing; **wsr** = wrong side row; **yfwd** = yarn forward; **yrh** = yarn round hook; **yon** = yarn over needle. Special abbreviations also appear with the patterns to which they belong.

Tension

Each pattern comes with specific tension instructions in a box. It is very important to work to the correct tension in order to obtain the correct size and appearance. Always knit a tension square before you begin the pattern. If your square is smaller than specified you will need to use thicker needles. If your square is larger you will need to use thinner needles.

Sizes and Measurements

The sizes given for each pattern are only approximate. It is always best to measure your child and refer to the garment measurements to choose the correct size.
Note: Figures in brackets refer to the larger sizes. Where only one number appears it applies to all sizes.

Knitting Needles Conversion Chart

Metric (mm)	2.25	2.75	3	3.25	3.75	4
English	13	12	11	10	9	8
US		0	1	2	3	4	5

When knitting with set 4 double pointed needles, divide stitches equally over 3 needles and use remaining needle to knit off stitches. Each needle is used in turn to knit off.

Joining Knitting

Which method of joining knitting you choose can greatly affect the final result. There are 2 commonly used methods. The edge to edge method gives an almost invisible seam and is ideal for lightweight knits, baby clothes and attaching button and buttonhole bands. Place the pieces to be joined right side up and edge to edge, matching rows. Fasten the yarn to the lower edge of the right hand piece then pick up the loop between the first and second stitch on the first row of the left hand piece. Now pick up the loop between the first and second stitches on the next row of the right hand piece. Continue in this way until the seam is complete.

The backstitch method provides a very strong join but one which does leave a ridge. Place the pieces to be joined with right sides together and rows and patterns matching. Sew along the seam, one stitch from the edge, using a firm but not tight backstitch.

Joining in a New Yarn

It is generally best not to join yarns by knotting except where the join falls at the end of a row. For all mid row joins a much smoother finish can be obtained by using the double strand method: work the last stitch to be worked in the old yarn and then allow it to fall to the back of the work. Insert the right hand needle into the next stitch on the left hand needle leaving a short tail. Knit the stitch in the usual way and then work 2 or 3 more stitches using the new yarn doubled. (On the next row treat these as single stitches.) On the wrong side trim the end of the new yarn and darn in the end of the old yarn for a neat finish.

Multi Coloured Knitting

Working with more than one colour adds a new dimension to your knitting. The simplest of these is a horizontal stripe pattern in two or more colours. The different yarns should be changed over at the right hand edge. Providing the stripes are narrow and only 2 or 3 colours are being used the yarns can be carried up the right hand side of the work without having to break off and rejoin a colour every time it is needed.

Where 2 colours are used repeatedly in the same row but not more than 5 stitches apart the best way to carry the different yarns is by stranding. This involves carrying the yarns loosely at the back of the work. Where the yarn needs to be carried over more than 5 stitches or if there are 3 or more colours it is best to use the weaving method where the yarn not being used is woven through the back of the work.

For changing colours when knitting large blocks of colour, such as in picture knitting, the yarns must be twisted quite tightly at the back of the work at each colour change. This is the intarsia method and depends on this twisting to ensure that there are no holes at the joins. When the piece is complete loose ends are darned in on the wrong side.

Where a number of colours are being used in a single row it is best to invest in some knitting bobbins. These are quite inexpensive plastic holders which keep the various strands of yarn from tangling together as you work.

Working from a Graph

Where a picture or pattern needs to be worked it is often given in the form of a graph or chart where each square represents one stitch and one row of knitting. Knit rows on the graph are worked from right to left and purl rows from left to right. The various colours to be worked are usually indicated by different symbols and care should be taken to work exactly as the graph indicates, perhaps by ticking off rows as they are completed.

First Aid

A dropped stitch which has caused a ladder is quite simple to deal with providing you have a crochet hook handy. Simply use the hook to knit or purl each stitch up the ladder until you reach the row on the needle. It is very important to pick up the stitches knitwise in the knit rows and purlwise in the purl rows.

Even the most expert knitter will occasionally knit a purl stitch or purl a knit one. It is quite easy to correct errors like this without resorting to unravelling the whole section. The simplest way is to drop the stitch immediately above the one to be changed and allow it to ladder down to it. Then with your crochet hook it is quite a simple matter to work back up to the needle again.

If you do need to unravel part of your work it is easier to pick up the loops again on a needle a couple of sizes smaller than the ones actually required. The smaller needles will slide easily into the loops without stretching them.

Blocking and Pressing

Before a garment can be completed it is usual for the pieces to be pressed and sometimes blocked. Ribbing is never pressed or blocked in order to retain its elasticity and highly textured patterns rarely are. Stocking stitch is usually pressed and often blocked. Be guided by the pattern instructions and the information on the paper band around the balls of yarn.

Blocking involves the "pinning out" of a piece of knitting to its correct shape and size on a padded surface. When pinning is complete and the measurements checked spray the piece evenly with cold water and allow it to dry completely.

Some knitted pieces will require pressing on the wrong side with a damp cloth and an iron temperature suitable for the yarn fibre. Never slide the iron to and fro across the knitting as this tends to distort the shape. It is enough to place the iron on the knitting and then lift it straight up before placing it down on another area.

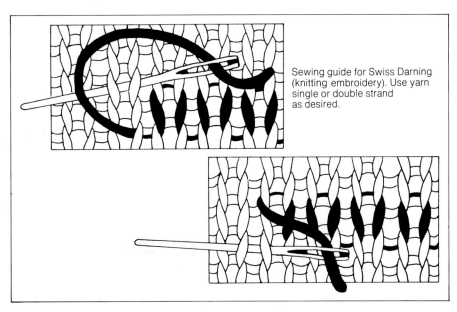

Sewing guide for Swiss Darning (knitting embroidery). Use yarn single or double strand as desired.

Classics in Colour

Chase away the winter blues with stripes
galore and charming checks in easy to knit 8 ply or
thrill your young man about town with the vibrant
colours of Salute the Flag. Knit up the boldly
geometric Harlequin to bring a smile to any child's
face. The pretty pastels of Star Struck, in delicate
5 ply, will dress up your little one for a
special occasion.

SALUTE THE FLAG
Jumper

To fit ages 6yrs, 8yrs, 10yrs

Materials

Cleckheaton 8 ply Wool Blend Crepe
50g balls
Main Colour (MC)   5 (6,7) balls
1 ball each of 5 colours
(C1, C2, C3, C4 and C5)
One pair each 4mm and 3.25mm needles,
one set of four 3.25mm needles, 2 stitch
holders, bobbins.

Measurements

Garment measures	76	83	90	cm
Back length (approx)	44	48	53	cm
Sleeve seam (approx)	32	36	40	cm

TENSION

22 sts to 10 cm over st st on 4mm
needles.
**IT IS IMPORTANT TO KNIT A
TENSION SQUARE AND TO
WORK TO STATED TENSION IN
ORDER TO OBTAIN REQUIRED
MEASUREMENTS. IF YOUR
SQUARE IS BIGGER USE FINER
NEEDLES. IF YOUR SQUARE IS
SMALLER USE THICKER
NEEDLES.**

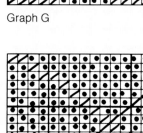

- ⊡ C1
- ╱ C2
- ☑ C3
- ☐ C4
- ⊙ C5
- ☒ MC

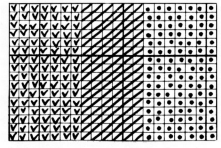

Graph A

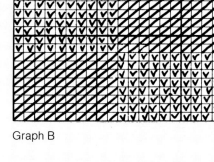

Graph B

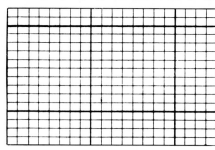

Graph C

Graph D

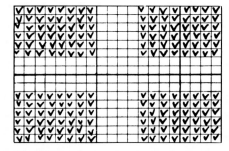

Graph E

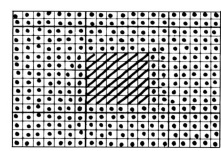

Graph F

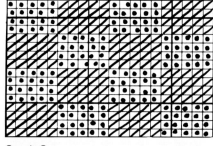

Graph G

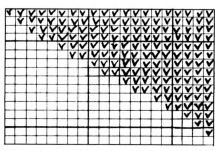

Graph H

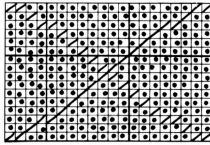

Graph I

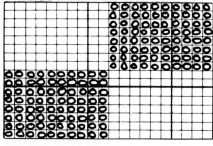

Graph J

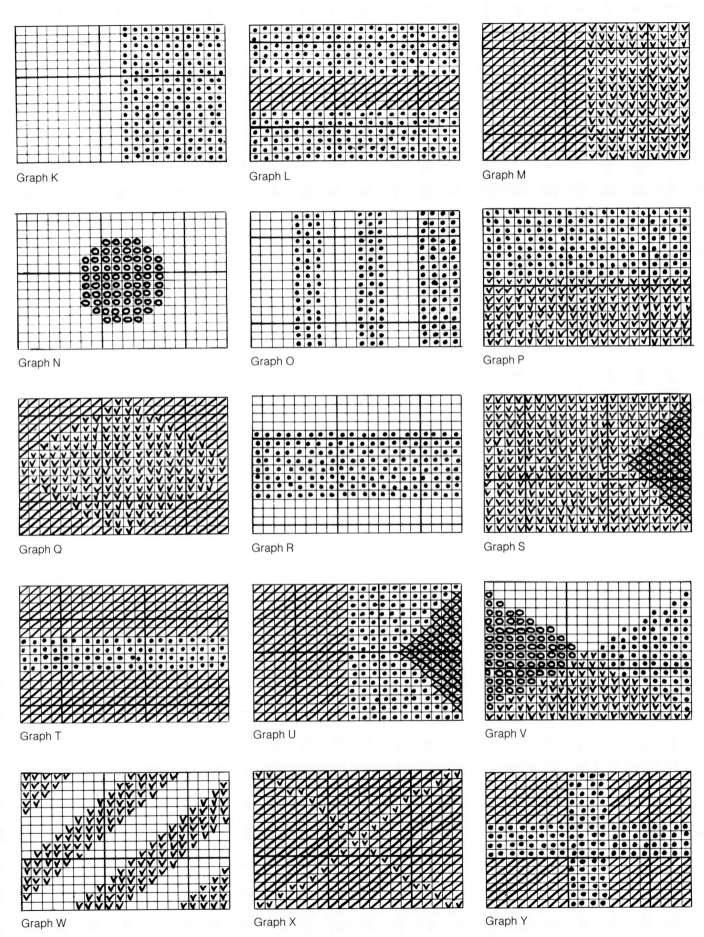

Graph K

Graph L

Graph M

Graph N

Graph O

Graph P

Graph Q

Graph R

Graph S

Graph T

Graph U

Graph V

Graph W

Graph X

Graph Y

Back

Using 3.25mm needles and MC, cast on 79 (87,93) sts.
1st row: k2, *p1, k1, rep from * to last st, k1.
2nd row: k1, *p1, k1, rep from * to end.
Rep 1st and 2nd rows until band meas 5 (6,6) cm from beg, ending with a 2nd row and inc 7 sts evenly across last row. 86 (94,100) sts.
Change to 4mm needles.
Work 2 (4,12) rows st st. * * * *
* * **Next row:** k33 (37,40) MC, work 1st row of Graph A, k33, (37,40) MC.
Next row: p33 (37,40), MC, work 2nd row of Graph A, p33 (37,40) MC.
Keeping Graph A correct, work 14 rows. * * *
Next row: k5 (9,12), MC, work 1st row of Graph B, k36MC, work 1st row of Graph C, k5 (9,12) MC.
Keeping Graphs B and C correct, work 15 rows.* *
Rep from * * to * * twice, then from * * to * * * once, working from Graphs in alphabetical order: e.g. Graph D in place of Graph A, Graphs E and F in place of Graphs B and C, etc.
Using MC, work 0 (4,10) rows st st.

Shape shoulders
Cast off 9 (10,10) sts at beg of next 4 rows, then 8 (9,11) sts at beg of foll 2 rows.
Leave rem 34 (36,38) sts on a stitch holder.

Front

Work as for Back to * * * *.
* * * * * **Next row:** k5 (9,12) MC, work 1st row of Graph K, k36 MC, work 1st row of Graph L, k5 (9,12) MC.
Keeping Graphs K and L correct, work 15 rows.
Next row: k33 (37,40) MC, work 1st row of Graph M, k33 (37,40) MC.
Keeping Graph M correct, work 15 rows. * * * * *

Shape neck
Next row: patt 34 (38,41), turn.
Keeping Graph T correct, then rem in st st, dec one st at neck edge in every row 6 (6,8) times, then in alt rows until 26 (29,31) sts rem.
Work 3 (3,5) rows.

Shape shoulders
Cast off 9 (10,10) sts at beg of next row and foll alt row.
Work 1 row. Cast off.
Slip next 18 sts onto a stitch holder and leave. Join MC to rem sts and keeping Graph U correct, complete other side of neck to correspond.

Left Sleeve

Using 3.25mm needles and MC, cast on 37 (37,39) sts.
Work 5 (6,6) cm rib as for lower band of Back, ending with a 2nd row and inc 7 (9,11) sts evenly across last row. 44 (46,50) sts.
Change to 4mm needles.
Cont in st st, inc one st at each end of 5th row and foll 4th rows until there are 50 (54,62) sts.
Work 3 rows st st.
Next row: inc in first st, k14 (16,20) MC, work 1st row of Graph V, k14 (16,20) MC, inc in last st. 52 (56,64) sts.
Keeping Graph V correct, work 31 rows (noting that Graph will be completed in foll 15th rows) AT SAME TIME, inc one st at each end of foll 6th (4th, 4th) rows until there are 62 (66,72) sts, **2nd and 3rd Sizes Only** — then in foll 6th rows until there are (68,76) sts. * * * * * *
Next row: (inc in first st) 0 (1,0) time / s, k21 (23,28) MC, work 1st row of Graph W, k21 (23,28) MC, (inc in last st) 0 (1,0) time / s. 62 (70,76) sts.
Keeping Graph W correct, work 29 (35,37) rows (noting that Graph will be completed in foll 15th rows) AT SAME TIME, inc one st at each end of 4th (6th,2nd) row and foll 6th rows until there are 66 (76,84) sts.

Shape sleeve top
Using MC, cast off 8 (9,10) sts at beg of next 6 rows. Cast off.

Right Sleeve

Work as for Left Sleeve to * * * * * *, working from Graph X instead of Graph V.
Next row: (inc in first st) 0 (1,0) time / s, k33 (35,40) MC, work 1st row of Graph Y, k9 (11,16), (inc in last st) 0 (1,0) time / s. 62 (70,76) sts.
Keeping placement of Graph Y correct, complete as for Left Sleeve.

Neckband

Using back stitch, join shoulder seams.
With rsf, using set of 3.25mm needles and MC, beg at left shoulder seam knit up 78 (84,90) sts evenly around neck edge, including sts from stitch holders.
1st round: *k1, p1, rep from * to end.
Rep 1st round 7 (8,8) times.
Cast off loosely in rib.

To Make Up

Tie coloured threads 16 (18,20) cm down from each shoulder seam. Using backstitch, sew in sleeves between coloured threads, placing centre of sleeves to shoulder seams. Join side and sleeve seams.

It is generally best not to join yarns by knotting except where the join falls at the end of a row. For all mid row joins a much smoother finish can be obtained by using the double strand method: work the last stitch to be worked in the old yarn and then allow it to fall to the back of the work. Insert the right hand needle into the next stitch on the left hand needle leaving a short tail. Knit the stitch in the usual way and then work 2 or 3 more stitches using the new yarn doubled. (On the next row treat these as single stitches.) On the wrong side trim the end of the new yarn and darn in the end of the old yarn for a neat finish.

For changing colours when knitting large blocks of colour, such as in picture knitting, the yarns must be twisted quite tightly at the back of the work at each colour change. This is the intarsia method and depends on this twisting to ensure that there are no holes at the joins. When the piece is complete loose ends are darned in on the wrong side.

STRIPES GALORE
Jumper

To fit ages 4yrs, 6yrs, 8yrs, 10yrs

Materials

Panda Magnum 8 ply 100 g balls
Main Colour (MC) (jade)	1 (1,1,1) ball
1st Contrast (C1) (royal blue)	1 (1,1,1) ball
2nd Contrast (C2) (red)	1 (1,1,1) ball
3rd Contrast (C3) (blue)	1 (1,1,1) ball
4th Contrast (C4) (orange)	1 (1,1,1) ball
5th Contrast (C5) (yellow)	1 (1,1,1) ball

One pair each 4mm and 3.25mm needles, 4 buttons.

Measurements

Garment				
measures	70	77	84	91 cm
Back length	46	50	54	58 cm
Sleeve seam	30	35	40	43 cm

TENSION
22 sts and 30 rows to 10 cm over st st on 4mm needles.
IT IS IMPORTANT TO KNIT A TENSION SQUARE AND TO WORK TO STATED TENSION IN ORDER TO OBTAIN REQUIRED MEASUREMENTS. IF YOUR SQUARE IS BIGGER USE FINER NEEDLES. IF YOUR SQUARE IS SMALLER USE THICKER NEEDLES.

Back

Using 3.25mm needles and MC, cast on 79 (87,95,103) sts.
1st row: k1, * p1, k1, rep from * to end.
2nd row: p1, * k1, p1, rep from * to end.
Rep last 2 rows until work meas 5 (5,6,6) cm from beg, ending with 2nd row.
Change to 4mm needles.
Work 24 rows st st in stripes of 7 rows C1, 2 rows C2, 2 rows C1, 2 rows C3, 2 rows C4, 2 rows C1, 2 rows MC, 2 rows C5, 2 rows C2 and 1 rows C3.
NOTE: When working in Fair Isle carry colour not in use loosely across on wrong side of work. Always carry colours to end of row.
25th row: k3 C3, * k1 C5, k3 C3, rep from * to end.
26th row: p2 C3, * p3 C5, p1 C3, rep from * to last st, p1 C3.
27th row: as for 25th row.
Work 14 rows st st (beg with a p row) in stripes of 1 row C3, 2 rows C2, 7 rows C1, 2 rows C2 and 2 rows C4.
42nd row: p1 C4, * p1 MC, p1 C4, rep from * to end.
Work 17 rows st st in stripes of 2 rows each C4, C1, C3, C4, C1, MC, C5, C2 and 1 row C3.
60th row: work as for 25th row, working p in place of k.
61st row: work as for 26th row, working k in place of p.
62nd row: as for 60th row.
Work 12 rows st st in stripes of 1 row C3, 2 rows C2, 7 rows C1 and 2 rows C2.
75th row: k1 C2, * k1 C5, k1 C2, rep from * to end.
Work 18 rows st st (beg with a p row) in stripes of 2 rows each C2, C1, C3, C4, C1, MC, C5, C2 and C4.
94th row: as for 42nd row.
Work 4 rows st st in stripes of 2 rows each C4 and C2.
These 98 rows form patt. Cont in patt until work measures 42 (46,49,53) cm from beg, working last row with wsf.
Using C1, **next row:** k. **
Work 11 (11,15,15) rows rib as before, beg with 2nd row.
Next row: rib 20 (23,26,29), cast off next 39 (41,43,45) sts loosely in rib, rib to end.
Work 11 (11,15,15) rows rib on last 20 (23,26,29) sts.
Cast off loosely in rib. With wsf, join C1 to rem sts and work 11 (11,15,15) rows rib.
Cast off loosely in rib.

Front

Work as for Back to **.
Work 5 (5,7,7) rows rib as before, beg with 2nd row.
Next row: rib 4 (6,6,8), cast off 2 sts, rib 9 (10,13,14), cast off 2 sts, rib 45 (47,49,51), cast off 2 sts, rib 9 (10,13,14), cast off 2 sts, rib 4 (6,6,8).
Next row: rib 4 (6,6,8), cast on 2 sts, rib 9 (10,13,14), cast on 2 sts, rib 45 (47,49,51), cast on 2 sts, rib 9 (10,13,14), cast on 2 sts, rib 4 (6,6,8). Work 4 (4,6,6) rows rib.
Cast off loosely in rib.

Sleeves

Using 3.25mm needles and MC, cast on 37 (39,41,43) sts. Work 5 (5,6,6) cm rib as for Back, ending with 2nd row and inc 6 (6,8,10) sts evenly across last row. 43 (45,49,53) sts.
Change to 4mm needles.
Working throughout in patt as for Back, inc one st at each end of 5th and foll 4th rows until there are 73 (81,91,99) sts.
Cont without further inc until work measures 30 (35,40,43) cm from beg, working last row with wsf.
Cast off.

To Make Up

Place last 12 (12,16,16) rows of Back under last 12 (12,16,16) rows of Front at shoulder and catch together at armhole edge. Tie markers to sides of Back and Front 17 (19,21,23) cm down from cast-off edge of front. Sew in sleeves between markers, placing centre of sleeves to cast-off edge of Front. Join side and sleeve seams. Sew buttons in position.

It is generally best not to join yarns by knotting except where the join falls at the end of a row. For all mid row joins a much smoother finish can be obtained by using the double strand method: work the last stitch to be worked in the old yarn and then allow it to fall to the back of the work. Insert the right hand needle into the next stitch on the left hand needle leaving a short tail. Knit the stitch in the usual way and then work 2 or 3 more stitches using the new yarn doubled. (On the next row treat these as single stitches.) On the wrong side trim the end of the new yarn and darn in the end of the old yarn for a neat finish.

HARLEQUIN
Jumper

To fit ages 4yrs, 6yrs, 8yrs, 10yrs

Materials

Panda Magnum   100g balls 8 ply
Main Colour (MC)   1 (2,2,2) ball/s
1 ball each 4 contrast
colours (C1, C2, C3 and
C4)
One pair each 3.25mm and 4mm
needles, 2 stitch holders.

Measurements

Garment				
measures	70	77	84	91 cm
Back length	46	50	54	58 cm
Sleeve seam	30	34	38	41 cm

TENSION

22 sts and 30 rows to 10 cm over
st st on 4mm needles.
**IT IS IMPORTANT TO KNIT A
TENSION SQUARE AND TO
WORK TO STATED TENSION IN
ORDER TO OBTAIN REQUIRED
MEASUREMENTS. IF YOUR
SQUARE IS BIGGER USE FINER
NEEDLES. IF YOUR SQUARE IS
SMALLER USE THICKER
NEEDLES.**

Back

Using 3.25mm needles and C1, cast on
79 (87,95,103) sts.
1st row: k2, * p1, k1 rep from * to last
st, k1.
2nd row: k1, * p1, k1 rep from * to end.
Rep last 2 rows until work meas 5
(5,6,6) cm from beg, ending with 2nd
row.
Change to 4mm needles.
Using C2, work 2 rows st st.
NOTE: When changing colour in centre of
row, twist the colour to be used
underneath and to the right of colour just
used to avoid making holes. Use a
separate ball of yarn for each section of
colour. Divide colours into smaller balls
as required.
3rd row: k5 (7,7,9) C2, k1 MC, k33
(35,39,41) C2, k1 MC, k33 (35,39,41) C2,
k1 MC, k5 (7,7,9) C2.

4th row and foll alt rows: p colours as
they appear.
5th row: k4 (6,6,8) C2, k3 MC, k31
(33,37,39) C2, k3 MC, k31 (33,37,39) C2,
k3 MC, k4 (6,6,8) C2.
7th row: k3 (5,5,7) C2, k5 MC, k29
(31,35,37) C2, k5 MC, k29 (31,35,37) C2,
k5 MC, k3 (5,5,7) C2.
9th row: k2 (4,4,6) C2, k7 MC, k27
(29,33,35) C2, k7 MC, k27 (29,33,35) C2,
k7 MC, k2 (4,4,6) C2.
Cont in this manner moving colours over
in alt rows until the row "p22 (25,27,30)
MC, p1 C2, p33 (35,39,41) MC, p1 C2,
p22 (25,27,30) MC" has been worked.
Using MC, work 2 rows st st.
Next row: k22 (25,27,30) MC, k1 C3, k33
(35,39,41) MC, k1 C3, k22 (25,27,30)
MC.
Next row: p colours as they appear.
Next row: k21 (24,26,29) MC, k3 C3, k31
(33,37,39) MC, k3 C3, k21(24,26,29) MC.
Next row: p colours as they appear.
Next row: k20 (23,25,28) MC, k5 C3, k29
(31,35,37) MC, k5 C3, k20 (23,25,28)
MC.
Cont in this manner moving colours over
in alt rows until the row "p5 (7,7,9) C3, p1
MC, p33 (35,39,41) C3, p1 MC, p33
(35,39,41) C3, p1 MC, p5 (7,7,9) C3" has
been worked.
Work 20 rows st st in stripes of 8 rows
each C3 and C2, then 4 rows C4.
Using MC, cont until work meas 46
(50,54,58) cm from beg, working last row
with wsf.
Next row: cast off 26 (29,32,35) sts, k27
(29,31,33), cast off last 26 (29,32,35) sts.
Leave rem sts on stitch holder.

Front

Work throughout in patt as for Back until
there are 22 (24,26,28) rows less than
Back to shoulder.

Shape neck
Next row: k32 (36,40,44), turn.
Cont on these 32 (36,40,44) sts. Dec one
st at neck edge in alt rows until 26
(29,32,35) sts rem.
Work 9 rows. Cast off.
With rsf, sl next 15 sts onto a stitch holder
and leave. Join MC to rem sts and work
other side to correspond.

Sleeves

Using 3.25mm needles and C1, cast on
37 (39,41,43) sts. Work 5 (5,6,6) cm rib
as for Back, ending with 2nd row and inc
4 (8,6,12) sts evenly across last row. 41
(47,47,55) sts.
Change to 4mm needles.
Using MC and working in st st inc one st

at each end of 3rd and foll alt (4th,4th,4th)
row/s until there are 45 (53,61,67) sts.
Work 1 (3,3,3) row/s.
Next row: inc in MC in first st, k4 (7,9,11)
MC, k1 C3, k33 (35,39,41) MC, k1 C3, k4
(7,9,11) MC, inc in MC in last st. 47
(55,63,69) sts.
Next row: p colours as they appear.
Next row: k5 (8,10,12) MC, k3 C3, k31
(33,37,39) MC, k3 C3, k5 (8,10,12) MC.
Next row: p colours as they appear.
Next row: inc in MC in first st, k3 (6,8,10)
MC, k5 C3, k29 (31,35,37) MC, k5 C3, k3
(6,8,10) MC, inc in MC in last st. 49
(57,65,71) sts.
Cont moving colours over in alt rows, AT
SAME TIME inc at each end of foll 4th
rows until there are 63 (71,81,89) sts.
Work 0 (2,2,0) rows.
Next row: p0 (0,1,3) MC, p31 (35,39,41)
C3, p1 MC, p31 (35,39,41) C3, p0 (0,1,3)
MC. Work 20 rows st st in stripes of 8
rows each C3 and C2, then 4 rows C4,
AT SAME TIME inc one st at each end of
foll 4th rows from previous inc until there
are 73 (81,91,99) sts. Using MC, cont
without further inc until work meas 30
(34,38,41) cm from beg, working last row
with wsf.
Cast off.

Neckband

Join right shoulder seam. With rsf, using
3.25mm needles and MC, pick up 85
(91,97,103) sts evenly around neck,
including sts from stitch holders.
Using C1, **next row:** p.
Work 6 (6,8,8) rows rib as for Back.
Cast off loosely in rib.

To Make Up

Join left shoulder and neckband seam.
Tie markers to sides of Back and Front 17
(19,21,23) cm down from shoulder
seams. Sew in sleeves between markers,
placing centre of sleeves to shoulder
seams. Join side and sleeve seams. If
desired, cut C1 into 10 cm lengths and
using 2 strands tog, tie a knot in each st
in first row of C2 stripe where illustrated.
Trim fringe.

OXFORD BLUES
Cardigan

To fit ages 2yrs, 4yrs, 6yrs

Materials

Cleckheaton 8 ply Machine Wash 50g balls
Main Colour (MC)   3 (4,5) balls
1st Contrast (C1)   2 balls
2nd Contrast (C2)   1 ball
3rd Contrast (C3)   1 ball
One pair each 4mm and 3.25mm
needles, 2 stitch holders, 7 buttons.

Measurements

Garment measures	63	69	75	cm
Back length	36	40	44	cm
Sleeve seam	21.5	26	31.5	cm

TENSION
22 sts to 10 cm over st st, using
4mm needles.
**IT IS IMPORTANT TO KNIT A
TENSION SQUARE AND TO
WORK TO STATED TENSION IN
ORDER TO OBTAIN REQUIRED
MEASUREMENTS. IF YOUR
SQUARE IS BIGGER USE FINER
NEEDLES. IF YOUR SQUARE IS
SMALLER USE THICKER
NEEDLES.**

Back

Using 3.25mm needles and MC, cast on
71 (77,85) sts.
1st row: k2, *p1, k1, rep from * to last
st, k1.
2nd row: k1, *p1, k1, rep from * to end.
Rep 1st and 2nd rows 4 (6,7) times more.
Change to 4mm needles.**
Cont in st st and stripes throughout of 6
rows MC, 2 rows C2, 6 rows C1, 2 rows
C3, 6 rows MC and 2 rows C2, until work
meas 35 (39,43)cm from beg, ending
with a purl row.

Shape shoulders
Keeping stripes correct, cast off 8 (9,10)
sts at beg of next 4 rows, then 9 (10,11)
sts at beg of foll 2 rows.
Leave rem 21 (21,23) sts on a stitch
holder.

Left Front

Using 3.25mm needles and MC, cast on
35 (39,43) sts.
Work from ** to ** of back.
Cont in st st and stripes as given for back
until there are 15 (17,17) rows less than
back to shoulder shaping.

Shape neck
Keeping stripes correct —
Next row (wrong side): cast off 6 (6,7)
sts, purl to end.
Dec one st at end of next and foll alt rows
until 25 (28,31) sts rem.
Work 7 rows in stripes.
Shape shoulder
Cast off 8 (9,10) sts at beg of next row
and foll alt row.
Work 1 row.
Cast off.

Right Front

Work to correspond with left front,
reversing all shapings.

Sleeves

Using 3.25mm needles and MC, cast on
35 (37,39) sts.
Work 10 (14,14) rows in rib as given for
lower band, inc 6 (6,8) sts evenly across
last row. 41 (43,47) sts.
Change to 4mm needles.
Cont in st st and stripes as given for back,
inc one st each end of next row and foll
8th (6th, 6th) rows 4 (2,2) times, then in
foll 10th (8th,8th) row /s 1 (5,7) times. 53
(59,67) sts.
Keeping stripes correct, cont without
shaping until side edge meas 21.5
(26,31.5)cm from beg, ending with a purl
row.

Shape top
Keeping stripes correct, cast off 5 (5,6)
sts at beg of next 6 rows.
Cast off rem sts.

Left Front Band

Using 3.25mm needles and MC, cast on
11 sts. ***.
Work 95 (107,117) rows garter st – every
row knit (1st row is wrong side).
Break off yarn leave sts on a stitch holder

Right Front Band

Work as for Left Front Band to ***
Work 3 rows garter st (1st row is wrong
side).
Next row: k5, cast off 2 sts, k4.
Next row: k4, cast on 2 sts, k5. Knit 14
(16,18) rows.
Rep last 16 (18,20) rows 4 times more,
then buttonhole rows once. 6 buttonholes.
Knit 11 (13,15) rows. Do not break off yarn,
leave sts on needle.

Neckband

Using back stitch, join shoulder seams.
With rsf using 3.25mm needles holding
right front band sts and MC, knit up 65
(69,73) sts evenly around neck edge
(including sts from back stitch holder),
then knit across sts from left front band.
87 (91,95) sts.
Next row: k11, *p1, k1, rep from * to last
12 sts, p1, k11.
Keeping garter st. and rib correct, work 16
rows working a buttonhole (as before) in
3rd and 4th rows. Cast off loosely.

To Make Up

Tie coloured threads 12 (13,15) cm down
from each shoulder on back and fronts.
Using back stitch, sew in sleeves between
coloured threads. Sew up side and sleeve
seams. Sew front bands in position. Sew
on buttons.

The same basic technique is used to work buttonholes, lace patterns and eyelets. This involves positioning the yarn over or around the right hand needle and following this with a simple decrease. How the yarn is positioned generally depends on where it is to be worked. Between 2 knit stitches or between 2 purl and a knit stitch, the yarn is brought to the front of the work and then over the right hand needle ready to work the next knit stitch. This is shown in pattern instructions as "yfwd". Between 2 purl stitches or a knit and a purl stitch the yarn is wrapped around the right hand needle bringing it to the front again ready to work the next purl stitch. This is shown in pattern instructions as "yrn". With this very simple method you can work buttonholes, a row of eyelets or a picot edging for a baby's jacket.

A dropped stitch which has caused a ladder is quite simple to deal with providing you have a crochet hook handy. Simply use the hook to knit or purl each stitch up the ladder until you reach the row on the needle. It is very important to pick up the stitches knitwise in the knit rows and purlwise in the purl rows. Even the most expert knitter will occasionally knit a purl stitch or purl a knit one. It is quite easy to correct errors like this without resorting to unravelling the whole section. The simplest way is to drop the stitch immediately above the one to be changed and allow it to ladder down to it. Then with your crochet hook it is quite a simple matter to work back up to the needle again.

If you do need to unravel part of your work it is easier to pick up the loops again on a needle a couple of sizes smaller than the ones actually required. The smaller needles will slide easily into the loops without stretching them.

TANK TOP
Sleeveless Pullover

Materials

Yarn:	50 g balls 8 ply
Sizes:	12mths (18mths, 2yrs)

Instructions for 18mths and 2yrs are in brackets. When only one number appears it applies to all three sizes.

Main colour:	3(3,4) balls royal blue
Contrast:	small amount of navy, red and yellow

One pair each size 3mm and 3.75mm needles,

Garment Measures

Chest	49	54	59	cm
Length	29	31	34	cm

TENSION
24 sts and 31 rows to 10cm in st st using size 3.75mm needles.
IT IS IMPORTANT TO KNIT A TENSION SQUARE AND TO WORK TO STATED TENSION IN ORDER TO OBTAIN REQUIRED MEASUREMENTS. IF YOUR SQUARE IS BIGGER USE FINER NEEDLES. IF YOUR SQUARE IS SMALLER USE THICKER NEEDLES.

Back

Using 3mm needles and royal blue, cast on 60(66,72) sts and work in single rib for 3cm. Change to 3.75mm needles and cont in st st until work meas 17(19,21)cm from cast on edge.

Shape armholes
Cast off 3 sts at beg of next 2 rows, 2 sts at beg of foll 2 rows and 1 st each end of next row. (48,54,60) sts. Cont in st st until work meas 28(30,33)cm from cast on edge.

Shape shoulders
Cast off 5(6,7) sts at beg of next 4 rows. Cast off rem 28(30,32) sts.

Front

Using 3mm needles and royal blue wool, cast on 60(66,72) sts and work in single rib for 3cm.
Change to 3.75mm needles and cont in striped patt as follows:
2 rows royal blue, st st.
* 2 rows yellow, g st.
6 rows royal blue, st st.
2 rows red, g st.
6 rows royal blue, st st.
2 rows navy, g st.
6 rows royal blue, st st.
Rep from *.
Work in patt until work meas 17(19,21)cm from cast on edge.

Shape armholes
Cast off 3 sts at beg of next 2 rows, 2 sts at beg of foll 2 rows, and 1 st each end of next row. 48(54,60) sts.
Cont in patt for 2cm.

Shape neck
Divide sts evenly and work each side separately 24(27,30) sts. Cont in patt, dec 1 st at neck edge on alt rows 14(15,16) times. Cont in patt until work meas 29(31,34)cm from cast on edge.
Next row: cast off 5(6,7) sts.
Patt 1 row. Cast off rem 5(6,7) sts.

Neckband

Using 3mm needles and royal blue wool, cast on 110(120,130) sts and work in single rib for 2cm. Cast off loosely in rib.

Armhole Bands

Using 3mm needles and royal blue wool, cast on 86(92,100) sts and work in single rib for 2cm. Cast off loosely in rib.

To Make Up

Press each piece (except ribbing) with a warm iron and a damp cloth. Do not overpress. Sew side seams. Sew shoulder seams. Sew ends of armhole bands together and then on to armhole openings. Sew on neckband, crossing over the two ends and placing them at right angles to the V-neck.

CHARMING CHECKS
Jumper

To fit ages 4yrs, 6yrs, 8yrs

Materials

Panda Magnum	100g balls 8 ply
Main Colour (MC)	1 (1,2) ball/s
Contrast Colour (C1)	2 (2,2) balls

One pair each 3mm and 3.75mm needles, 2 stitch holders, 3 buttons.

Measurements

Garment measures	68	77	86	cm
Back length	37	42	46	cm
Sleeve seam	28	32	35	cm

TENSION

26 sts and 35 rows to 10 cm over st st on 3.75mm needles.
IT IS IMPORTANT TO KNIT A TENSION SQUARE AND TO WORK TO STATED TENSION IN ORDER TO OBTAIN REQUIRED MEASUREMENTS. IF YOUR SQUARE IS BIGGER USE FINER NEEDLES. IF YOUR SQUARE IS SMALLER USE THICKER NEEDLES.

Back

Using 3mm needles and MC, cast on 89 (101,113) sts.
1st row: k1, * p1, k1, rep from * to end.
2nd row: p1, * k1, p1, rep from * to end.
Rep 1st and 2nd rows until work meas 3 (4,5) cm from beg, ending with a 2nd row and inc one st in centre of last row. 90 (102,114) sts.
Change to 3.75mm needles.
NOTE: When working Fair Isle squares carry colour not in use loosely across on wrong side of work. When changing colour in middle of row, twist the colour to be used underneath and to the right of colour just used, drawing both ends up firmly to avoid holes. * *
Begin first patt.
1st row: k30 (34,38) C1, k2 MC (k2 C1,k2 MC) 7 (8,9) times, k30 (34,38) C1.
2nd row: p31 (35,39) C1, (p2 MC, p2 C1) 7 (8,9) times, p1 MC, p30 (34,38) C1.

3rd row: k32 (36,40) C1, (k2 MC, k2 C1) 7 (8,9) times, k30 (34,38) C1.
4th row: p30 (34,38) C1, p1 MC (p2 C1,p2 MC) 7 (8,9) times, p31 (35,39) C1.
These 4 rows form first patt.
Work 36 (40,44) more rows first patt.
Beg 2nd patt.
1st row: k2 C1, (k2 MC,k2 C1) 7 (8,9) times, k30 (34,38) MC, k2 C1, (k2 MC,k2 C1) 7 (8,9) times.
2nd row: p1 MC, (p2 C1,p2 MC) 7 (8,9) times, p1 C1, p31 (35,39) MC, (p2 C1,p2 MC) 7 (8,9) times, p1 C1.
3rd row: k2 MC, (k2 C1,k2 MC) 7 (8,9) times, k32 (36,40) MC, (k2 C1,k2 MC) 7 (8,9) times.
4th row: p1 C1, (p2 MC,p2 C1) 7 (8,9) times, p31 (35,39) MC, p1 C1, (p2 MC,p2 C1) 7 (8,9) times, p1 MC.
These 4 rows form 2nd patt.
Work 36 (40,44) more rows 2nd patt.
Work 40 (44,48) rows first patt.
Next row: Using C1, cast off 27 (31,35) sts; using MC, k to last 27 (31,35) sts; using C1, cast off last 27 (31,35) sts.
Leave rem 36 (40,44) sts on stitch holder.

Front

Work as for back to * *.
Beg first patt:
Work 40 (44,48) rows as for 2nd patt of Back, using MC in place of C1 and C1 in place of MC.
Beg 2nd patt:
Work 40 (44,48) rows as for 1st patt of Back, using MC in place of C1 and C1 in place of MC.
Work 22 (24,26) rows as for 2nd patt of Back, using MC in place of C1 and C1 in place of MC.

Shape neck
Keeping patt correct,
Next row: patt 35 (41,47), turn.
Cont on these 35 (41,47) sts. Dec one st at neck edge in each of next 8 (10,12) rows. 27 (31,35) sts. Work 9 rows. Using MC, cast off. With rsf, sl next 20 sts onto stitch holder and leave.
Join yarn to rem sts and patt to end of row.
Dec one st at neck edge in each of next 8 (10,12) rows. 27 (31,35) sts.
Work 9 rows.
Using MC, cast off.

Right Sleeve

Using 3mm needles and MC, cast on 49 (51,53) sts. Work 3 (4,5) cm rib as for Back, ending with a 2nd row and inc 3 (1,7) sts evenly across last row. 52 (52,60) sts.

Change to 3.75mm needles.
Begin first patt. * *
1st row: k2 C1, (k2 MC,k2 C1) 6 (6,7) times, k26 (26,30) MC.
2nd row: p27 (27,31) MC, (p2 C1,p2 MC) 6 (6,7) times, p1 C1.
3rd row: k2 MC, (k2 C1,k2 MC) 6 (6,7) times, k26 (26,30) MC.
4th row: p26 (26,30) MC, p1 C1 (p2 MC,p2 C1) 6 (6,7) times, p1 MC.
*** These 4 rows form first patt.
Keeping patt correct, inc one st at each end of next and alt rows until there are 56 (68,72) sts, then in foll 4th rows until there are 72 (80,88) sts, introducing appropriate coloured blocks at side when 30 (34,38) sts are reached in 2 centre blocks.
Work 1 row. ***
Beg 2nd patt.
1st row: k2 MC, k2 C1, k2 MC, k30 (34,38) C1, k2 MC, (k2 C1,k2 MC) 7 (8,9) times, k6 C1.
2nd row: p7 C1, (p2 MC,p2 C1) 7 (8,9) times, p1 MC, p31 (35,39) C1, p2 MC, p2 C1, p1 MC.
Keeping patt correct as placed in last 2 rows, inc one st at each end of next and foll 4th rows until there are 86 (96,106) sts.
Work 13 rows straight.
Cast off.

Left Sleeve

Work as for Right sleeve to * *.
1st row: k26 (26,30) MC, k2 C1, (k2 MC,k2 C1) 6 (6,7) times.
2nd row: p1 MC, (p2 C1,p2 MC) 6 (6,7) times, p1 C1, p26 (26,30) MC.
3rd row: k28 (28,32) MC, (k2 C1,k2 MC) 6 (6,7) times.
4th row: p1 C1, (p2 MC,p2 C1) 6 (6,7) times, p27 (27,31) MC.
Work as for Right Sleeve from *** to ***.
Beg 2nd patt.
1st row: k8 C1, (k2 MC,k2 C1) 7 (8,9) times, k32 (36,40) C1, k2 MC, k2 C1.
2nd row: p1 C1, p2 MC, p2 C1, p31 (35,39) C1, p1 C1, (p2 MC,p2 C1) 7 (8,9) times, p1 MC, p6 C1.
Keeping patt correct as placed in last 2 rows, complete as for Right Sleeve.

Neckband

Join right shoulder seam. With rsf, using 3mm needles and MC, pick up 10 (12,14) sts evenly along left side of neck, k across sts from front stitch holder, dec 4 sts evenly across, pick up 17 (19,21) sts along right side of neck, then k across back stitch holder, dec 8 sts evenly across. 71 (79,87) sts.

Work 7 rows rib as for Back, beg with 2nd row.
Cast off in rib.

Front Shoulder Band

With rsf, using 3mm needles and MC, pick up 33 (37,41) sts evenly across left shoulder and end of neckband. Work 3 rows rib as for Back, beg with 2nd row.
Next row: rib 4, cast off 2 sts (rib 10 [12,14], cast off 2 sts) twice, rib 3.
Next row: rib 3, cast on 2 sts (rib 10 [12,14], cast on 2 sts) twice, rib 4.
Work 4 rows rib.
Cast off in rib.

Back Shoulder Band

Work to correspond with Front Shoulder Band, omitting buttonholes.

To Make Up

Sew buttons to Back Shoulder Band and fasten. Sew ends of shoulder bands tog at armhole edge. Sew sleeves in position, noting to match blocks to Back and Front as illustrated. Join side and sleeve seams.

Where a picture or pattern needs to be worked it is often given in the form of a graph or chart where each square represents one stitch and one row of knitting. Knit rows on the graph are worked from right to left and purl rows from left to right. The various colours to be worked are usually indicated by different symbols and care should be taken to work exactly as the graph indicates, perhaps by ticking off rows as they are completed.

STAR STRUCK
Dainty Dress

Materials

Yarn:	50g balls 5 ply
Sizes:	3mths (6mths, 12mths)

Instructions for 6mths and 12mths are in brackets. When only one number appears it applies to all sizes.
Quantity:
Main colour 4(5,5) balls white
Contrast 1(2,2) balls blue
One pair each 3mm and 3.75mm needles; 4 small white buttons; a few lengths of elastic thread.

Garment Measures

Chest	67	75	81	cm
Length	40	43	46	cm
Sleeve length	15	17	20	cm

TENSION
26 sts and 38 rows to 10cm in st st using 3.75mm needles.
IT IS IMPORTANT TO KNIT A TENSION SQUARE AND TO WORK TO STATED TENSION IN ORDER TO OBTAIN REQUIRED MEASUREMENTS. IF YOUR SQUARE IS BIGGER USE FINER NEEDLES. IF YOUR SQUARE IS SMALLER USE THICKER NEEDLES.

Stitches Used

Single rib:
1st row: k1 p1.
2nd row: knit and purl sts as they come.
Repeat first 2 rows.
Stocking stitch: 1 row knit, 1 row purl. Follow the graph for the design, taking care to cross over the yarns at the back of work when changing from one colour to another.

DRESS

Back

Using 3mm needles, white, cast on 110(120,128) sts. Work in st st for 2.5cm for hem, ending with wsr. Purl 1 row for foldline of Hem. Change to 3.75mm needles. Beg with purl row cont in st st in white only for 3cm, then commence to follow the graph. At same time dec 1 st at each end of next knit row and every following 10th knit row ten times. Cont until work meas 27(29,32)cm.

Shape Armholes
Cast off 3 sts at beg of next 2 rows. Dec 1 st at each end of next 5 knit rows. 74(84,92).
When work meas 29.5(31.5,34.5)cm change to 3mm needles and work in single rib, without shaping, until work measures 40(43,46)cm.

Shape neck
Rib 19(22,25) sts and place them on st holder. Cast off next 36(40,42) sts and rib to end of row. Work on these sts only for a further 1.5cm.

Buttonholes
Next row: rib 3, k2 tog, yon, rib 9(12,15), yon, k2 tog, rib 3. Cont in single rib as before. At 2.5cm from neck shaping cast off all sts.
Join yarn to sts on holder and complete other side reversing all shapings.

Front

Work as for back until garment measures 36(38,42)cm. Shape neck as for back but without buttonholes and casting off 3cm after neck shaping.

Sleeves

Using 3mm needles cast on 50(52,56) sts and work 4cm in single rib. Change to 3.75mm needles and begin following the graph. At same time inc 1 st at each end of every 8th row five times. 60(62,66) sts. Work until sleeve measures 15(17,20)cm from cast on edge.

Shape sleeve top
Dec 1 st at each end of next five knit rows. Cast off remaining 50(52,56) sts.

To Make Up

Sew up side seams. Fold hem to inside and neatly catch in place. Fold shoulder edges over one another but only sew them down at armhole edge. Sew on buttons. Thread 2 rows of elastic thread through cast off edges of back and front. Sew up sleeve seams. Sew in sleeves.

I = light blue
☐ = white

Classics in Texture

No child's wardrobe would be complete
without the traditional cables of that classic of
classics, an Aran sweater, or try Snowball, with its
chunky ribbed pattern, to be a hit on the slopes this
season. For something more delicate, try timeless
mohair or the delicate patterns in
Blossom or Look of Lace.

Classic Aran, page 29

CLASSIC ARAN
Cardigan

To fit ages 2yrs, 4yrs, 6yrs

Materials

Cleckheaton Country 8 ply 50g balls
　　　　　　　　　10 (11,12) balls
One pair each 4mm and 3.25mm
needles, 3 stitch holders, cable needle, 7
buttons.

Measurements

Garment measures	66	71	76	cm
Back length	38	42	44	cm
Sleeve seam	23	28	33	cm

TENSION

22 sts to 10cm over st st, using
4mm needles.
**IT IS IMPORTANT TO KNIT A
TENSION SQUARE AND TO
WORK TO STATED TENSION IN
ORDER TO OBTAIN REQUIRED
MEASUREMENTS. IF YOUR
SQUARE IS BIGGER USE FINER
NEEDLES. IF YOUR SQUARE IS
SMALLER USE THICKER
NEEDLES.**

SPECIAL ABBREVIATIONS

"C4F" = Slip next 2 sts onto cable
needle and leave at front of work, k2,
then k2 from cable needle.
"C4B" = Slip next 2 sts onto cable
needle and leave at back of work, k2,
then k2 from cable needle.
"T4B" = Slip next 2 sts onto cable
needle and leave at back of work, k2,
then p2 from cable needle.
"T4F" = Slip next 2 sts onto cable
needle and leave at front of work, p2,
then k2 from cable needle.
"BC" = Slip next st onto cable needle
and leave at back of work, k1tbl, then p1
from cable needle.
"FC" = Slip next st onto cable needle
and leave at front of work, p1, then k1tbl
from cable needle.
"TW" = Knit into front of second st on
left hand needle, then into front of first st,
slipping both sts off needle tog.

Pattern Panel A
(worked over 9 sts):
1st row: p3, k3tbl, p3.
2nd row: k3, p3tbl, k3.
3rd row: p2, "BC", k1tbl, "FC", p2.
4th row: k2, (p1tbl, k1) twice, p1tbl, k2.
5th row: p1, "BC", p1, k1tbl, p1, "FC", p1.
6th row: k1, (p1tbl, k2) twice, p1tbl, k1.
7th row: "BC", p1, k3tbl, p1, "FC".
8th row: p1tbl, k2, p3tbl, k2, p1tbl.
Rows 1 to 8 inclusive form Patt Panel A

Patt Panel B
(worked over 16 sts):
1st row: k2, p4, "C4B", p4, k2.
2nd row: p2, k4, p4, k4, p2.
3rd row: k2, p4, k4, p4, k2.
4th row: as 2nd row.
5th row: ("T4F", "T4B") twice.
6th row: as 3rd row.
7th row: as 2nd row.
8th row: as 3rd row.
9th row: p2, "C4B", p4, "C4B", p2.
10th row: as 3rd row.
11th row: as 9th row.
12th row: as 3rd row.
13th row: as 2nd row.
14th row: as 3rd row.
15th row: ("T4B", "T4F") twice.
16th row: as 2nd row.
17th row: as 3rd row.
18th row: as 2nd row.
19th row: as 1st row.
20th row: as 2nd row.
Rows 1 to 20 inclusive form Patt Panel B.

Patt Panel C
(worked over 12 sts):
1st row: "TW", p2, "C4F", p2, "TW".
2nd row: p2, k2, p4, k2, p2.
3rd row: "TW", p2, k4, p2, "TW".
4th row: as 2nd row.
Rows 1 to 4 inclusive form Patt Panel C.

Patt Panel D
(worked over 12 sts):
Work as for Patt Panel C, noting to work
"C4B" in place of "C4F".

Back

Using 3.25mm needles, cast on 77
(81,87) sts.
1st row: k2, *p1, k1, rep from * to last st,
k1.
2nd row: k1, *p1, k1, rep from * to end.
Rep 1st and 2nd rows until band meas
6cm from beg, ending with a 1st row.
Next row: rib 0 (1,5), (inc in next st, rib 2)
25 times, inc in next st, rib 1 (4,6). 103
(107,113) sts.
Change to 4mm needles.
1st row: k1 (3,6), p1, "TW", work 1st row
of Patt Panel A across next 9 sts, "TW",
p2, work 1st row of Patt Panel B across
next 16 sts, p2, work 1st row of Patt

Panel C across next 12 sts, work 1st row
of Patt Panel A across next 9 sts, work
1st row of Patt Panel D across next 12
sts, p2, work 1st row of Patt Panel B
across next 16 sts, p2, "TW", work 1st
row of Patt Panel A across next 9 sts,
"TW", p1, k1 (3,6).
2nd row: p1 (3,6), k1, p2, work 2nd row
of Patt Panel A across next 9 sts, p2, k2,
work 2nd row of Patt Panel B across next
16 sts, k2, work 2nd row of Patt Panel D
across next 12 sts, work 2nd row of Patt
Panel A across next 9 sts, work 2nd row
of Patt Panel C across next 12 sts, k2,
work 2nd row of Patt Panel B across next
16 sts, k2, p2, work 2nd row of Patt Panel
A across next 9 sts, p2, k1, p1 (3,6).
3rd row: k1 (3,6), p1, "TW", work 3rd
row of Patt Panel A across next 9 sts,
"TW", p2, work 3rd row of Patt Panel B
across next 16 sts, p2, work 3rd row of
Patt Panel C across next 12 sts, work 3rd
row of Patt Panel A across next 9 sts,
work 3rd row of Patt Panel D across next
12 sts, p2, work 3rd row of Patt Panel B
across next 16 sts, p2, "TW", work 3rd
row of Patt Panel A across next 9 sts,
"TW", p1, k1 (3,6).
4th row: p1 (3,6), k1 p2, work 4th row of
Patt Panel A across next 9 sts, p2, k2,
work 4th row of Patt Panel B across next
16 sts, k2, work 4th row of Patt Panel D
across next 12 sts, work 4th row of Patt
Panel A across next 9 sts, work 4th row
of Patt Panel C across next 12 sts, k2,
work 4th row of Patt Panel B across next
16 sts, k2, p2, work 4th row of Patt Panel
A across next 9 sts, p2, k1, p1 (3,6).
Keeping all patts correct, cont in patts as
placed in last 4 rows until work meas 37
(41,43)cm from beg, working last row on
wrong side.

Shape shoulders
Keeping patts correct, cast off 10 sts at
beg of next 4 (6,6) rows, then 9 (9,11) sts
at beg of foll 4 (2,2) rows.
Leave rem 27 (29,31) sts on a stitch
holder.

Pocket Linings
(make 2)

Using 4mm needles cast on 27 sts.
Work in st st until work meas 10cm from
beg, ending with a purl row, inc 4 sts
evenly across last row. 31 sts.
Leave sts on a stitch holder.

Left Front

Using 3.25mm needles, cast on 39
(41,43) sts.
Work in rib as given for lower band of
back, until band meas 6cm from beg,

ending with a 2nd row and inc 10 (10,11) sts evenly across last row. 49 (51,54) sts. Change to 4mm needles.**
1st row: k1 (3,6), p1, "TW", work 1st row of Patt.Panel A across next 9 sts, "TW", p2, work 1st row of Patt Panel B across next 16 sts, p2, work 1st row of Patt Panel C across next 12 sts, p2.
2nd row: k2, work 2nd row of Patt Panel C across next 12 sts, k2, work 2nd row of Patt Panel B across next 16 sts, k2, p2, work 2nd row of Patt Panel A across next 9 sts, p2, k1, p1 (3,6).
Keeping all patts correct, cont in patt until work meas 15cm from beg, working last row on wrong side.

Place pocket
1st row: k1 (3,6), p1, "TW", slip next 31 sts onto a stitch holder and leave, patt across sts from one stitch holder, patt 14. Cont in patt until there are 13 (13,15) rows less than back to shoulder shapings.

Shape neck
Keeping patts correct, cast off 6 (7,8) sts at beg of next row. Dec one st at neck in next and alt rows until 38 (39,41) sts rem. Work 3 (3,5) rows.

Shape shoulder
Keeping patt correct, cast off 10 sts at beg of next row and foll alt row, then 9 (10,10) sts at beg of foll alt row. Work 1 row.
Cast off.

Right Front

Work as given for left front to **.
1st row: p2, work 1st row of Patt Panel D across next 12 sts, p2, work 1st row of Patt Panel B across next 16 sts, p2, "TW", work 1st row of Patt Panel A across next 9 sts, "TW", p1, k1 (3,6). Cont in patts as placed in last row and complete to correspond with left front noting that row placing pocket reads thus — patt 14, slip next 31 sts onto stitch holder and leave, patt across sts from 2nd stitch holder, "TW", p1, k1 (3,6).

Sleeves

Using 3.25mm needles cast on 37 sts. Work in rib as given for lower band of back, until band meas 5cm from beg, ending with a 1st row.
Next row: rib 3, inc in each of next 32 sts, rib 2. 69 sts.
Change to 4mm needles.
1st row: work 1st row of Patt Panel B

across next 16 sts, p2, work 1st row of Patt Panel C across next 12 sts, work 1st row of Patt Panel A across next 9 sts, work 1st row of Patt Panel D across next 12 sts, p2, work 1st row of Patt Panel B across next 16 sts.
Keeping patt panels correct, as placed, cont in patt inc one st at each end of foll 4th rows until there are 79 (85,87) sts, then in foll 6th rows until there are 85 (91,97) sts, noting to work extra sts at each end into p2, "TW", then Patt Panel A.
Cont in patt without shaping, until side edge meas 23 (28,33)cm from beg, working last row on wrong side.

Shape top
Keeping patt correct, cast off 6 sts at beg of next 8 rows.
Cast off rem sts.

Right Front Band

With right side facing, using 3.25mm needles, knit up 101 (107,113) sts evenly along right front.
Work 3 rows rib as given for lower band of back, beg with a 2nd row.
Next row: rib 2 [cast off 2 sts, rib 15 (16,17)] 5 times, cast off 2 sts, rib 12 (13,14).
Next row: rib 12 (13,14), [cast on 2 sts, rib 15 (16,17)] 5 times, cast on 2 sts, rib 2. 6 buttonholes.
Work 4 rows rib.
Cast off loosely in rib.

Left Front Band

Work as for right band omitting buttonholes.

Neckband

Using back stitch, join shoulder seams. With right side facing using 3.25mm needles, knit up 69 (75,79) sts evenly around neck edge including side edge of front bands and sts from back neck stitch holder.
Work 3 rows rib as given for lower band of back, beg with a 2nd row.
Next row: rib 5, cast off 2 sts, rib to end.
Next row: rib to last 5 sts, cast on 2 sts, rib 5.
Work 2 rows rib.
Cast off loosely in rib.

Pocket Tops

With rsf, using 3.25mm needles, knit across sts from stitch holder.
Work 7 rows rib as given for lower band

of back, beg with a 2nd row.
Cast off loosely in rib.

To Make Up

Using back stitch, sew in sleeves placing centre of sleeves to shoulder seams. Join side and sleeve seams. Sew pocket linings and pocket tops in position. Sew on buttons.

CANDY FLOSS
Cardigan

To fit ages 4yrs, 6yrs, 8yrs

Materials

Hayfield 80% Luxury Mohair 50g balls
4 (5,5) balls
One pair each 4.50mm and 5.50mm
needles, stitch holders, 5 buttons.

Measurements

Garment measures	68	72	76	cm
Back length	33	37	41	cm
Sleeve seam	26	31	36	cm

TENSION

16 sts and 20 rows to 10 cm over
st st on 5.50mm needles.
**IT IS IMPORTANT TO KNIT A
TENSION SQUARE AND TO
WORK TO STATED TENSION IN
ORDER TO OBTAIN REQUIRED
MEASUREMENTS. IF YOUR
SQUARE IS BIGGER USE FINER
NEEDLES. IF YOUR SQUARE IS
SMALLER USE THICKER
NEEDLES.**

Back

Using 4.50mm needles, cast on 56 (60,64)
sts. Rib k1, p1 for 2.5 (3,3.5) cm.
Change to 5.50mm needles and st st and
work until back meas 20 (22,24) cm from
beg, ending with rsf.

Shape armholes
Cast of 2 (3,3) sts at beg of next 2 rows.
Dec 1 st each end of next and foll alt row.
48 (50,54) sts.
Cont straight until work meas 33
(37,41) cm from beg, ending with rsf.

Shape shoulders
Cast off 6 sts at beg of next 2 rows, then
cast off 6 (6,7) sts at beg of next 2 rows.
Slip rem sts on a holder.

Left Front

With 4.50mm needles, cast on 26 (28,30)
sts. Rib as for back.

Change to 5.50mm needles and st st and
work until front meas 20 (22,24) cm from
beg, ending with rsf.

Shape armhole
Cast off 2 (3,3) sts at beg of next row.
Work 1 row. Dec 1 st at armhole edge on
next and foll alt row. 22 (23,25) sts.
Cont straight until work meas 28 (32,36)
cm from beg, ending with rsf.

Shape neck
Cast off 3 (4,5) sts at beg of next row.
Work 1 row. Cast off 2 sts at beg of next
and foll alt rows 3 times in all, then dec 1
st at beg of foll alt row. 12 (12,13) sts.
Cont straight until front matches back to
shoulder, ending with a purl row.

Shape shoulder
Cast off 6 sts at beg of next row. Work 1
row. Cast off rem 6 (6,7) sts.

Right Front

Cast on and work as for Left Front,
shaping in reverse.

Sleeves

With 4.50 needles, cast on 30 (34,36) sts.
Rib as for back for 3 cm.
Change to 5.50mm needles and st st. Inc
1 st each end of 3rd and every foll 4th row
to 44 (50,56) sts.
Cont straight until work meas 24 (27,30)
cm from beg, ending with rsf.
Cast off loosely.

To Complete

Join shoulder seams using backstitch.

Neckband

With 4.50mm needles and rsf, pick up and
k46 (52,58) sts evenly around neck edge
(including sts from holder). Rib k1, p1 for
2.5 cm.
Cast off loosely in rib.

Right Front Band

With 4.50mm needles, cast on 53 (61,69)
sts. Work 2 rows rib as for back.
3rd row: rib 4, * cast off 2 sts, rib 9
(11,13), rep from * to last 5 sts, cast off 2
sts, rib 3.
4th row: rib 3, * cast on 2 sts, rib 9
(11,13), rep from * to last 6 sts, cast on 2

sts, rib 4. (5 buttonholes.)
Work 2 rows rib.
Cast off loosely in rib.

Left Front Band

Work as for Right Front Band, omitting
buttonholes.

To Make Up

Join side and sleeve seams. Sew in
sleeves. Sew cast off edge of front bands
in position. Sew on buttons. Do not press.

Which method of joining knitting
you choose can greatly affect the
final result. There are 2 commonly
used methods. The edge to edge
method gives an almost invisible
seam and is ideal for lightweight
knits, baby clothes and attaching
button and buttonhole bands. Place
the pieces to be joined right side up
and edge to edge, matching rows.
Fasten the yarn to the lower edge
of the right hand piece then pick up
the loop between the first and
second stitch on the first row of the
left hand piece. Now pick up the
loop between the first and second
stitches on the next row of the right
hand piece. Continue in this way
until the seam is complete.

The backstitch method provides
a very strong join but one which
does leave a ridge. Place the
pieces to be joined with right sides
together and rows and patterns
matching. Sew along the seam,
one stitch from the edge, using a
firm but not tight backstitch.

SNOWBALL
Polo-neck Sweater and Headband

Materials

Yarn: 25g balls 3ply
Sizes: 12mths (18mths, 2 yrs)
Instructions for 18mths and 2 years are in brackets. Where there is only one number it applies to all 3 sizes.
Quantity: 5(5,6) balls white 1(1,1) ball red
1 pair 2.75mm and 3mm knitting needles.
Set of 4 2.75mm double-pointed knitting needles.

Garment Measures

Chest	51	55	59	cm
Length to armhole	19	21	23	cm
Sleeve length to armhole	24	26	28	cm

TENSION
32 sts and 60 rows in pattern should measure 10cm square using 3mm needles.
IT IS IMPORTANT TO KNIT A TENSION SQUARE AND TO WORK TO STATED TENSION IN ORDER TO OBTAIN REQUIRED MEASUREMENTS. IF YOUR SQUARE IS BIGGER USE FINER NEEDLES. IF YOUR SQUARE IS SMALLER USE THICKER NEEDLES.

SWEATER

Back

Using 2.75mm needles and white wool cast on 84(90,96) sts and work in single rib for 4cm.
Change to 3mm needles and work in pattern as follows.
1st row: k to end of row.
2nd row: sl 1 purlwise, *p1, work a double st (yarn back, put point of right-hand needle into middle of next st in row below and k this st) * rep from * to * to last st, p1.
These 2 rows form the pattern. Work in pattern until work meas 19(21,23)cm from beg.

Shape armholes
Cast off 4 sts at the beg of the next 2 rows and 2 sts at beg of foll 4 rows. 68(74,80) sts. ** Cont in pattern until work meas 29(32,35)cm from beg.

Shape shoulders
Cast off 16(18,20) sts at beg of next 2 rows.
Slip the remaining 36(38,40) sts onto a st holder.

Front

Work as for back until **.
Cont in pattern until work meas 25(28,31)cm from beg.

Shape neck
With rsf, pattern 28(30,32) sts, slip these sts onto a st holder, cast off next 12(14,16) sts and work separately on remaining 28(30,32) sts, pattern to end.
Next row: pattern to end.
*Cast off 4 sts at beg (neck edge) of this row and 2 sts at beg (neck edge) of 4 following 4th rows.
16(18,20) sts. Cont in pattern until work meas 29(32,35)cm from beg.

Shape shoulder
Cast off remaining 16(18,20) sts. With rsf, join wool to outer edge of 28(30,32) sts left on st holder, pattern to end. Work as for right front neck from * to end.

Sleeves

Using 2.75mm needles and white wool cast on 70(74,78) sts and work in single rib for 8cm. Change to 3mm needles.
Next row: work in pattern as for back and front, increasing 1 st at both ends of this and the 8 following 8th(10th,12th) rows. 88(92,96) sts. Cont in pattern until work meas 24(26,28)cm from beg.

Shape sleeve top
Cast off 4 sts at beg of next 2 rows. (Work 2 rows patt straight, cast off 3 sts at beg of next 2 rows) twice, * work 2 rows patt straight, cast off 2 sts at beg of next 2 rows *, rep from * to * until 16 sts rem. Cont in pattern on rem 16 sts for 5(5.5,6)cm for saddle shoulder piece Leave sts on a st holder. These 16 sts form a part of polo collar.

To Make Up

Sew up side seams. Sew up sleeve seams. Sew in sleeves placing saddle shoulder piece between the back and front.

Polo-neck

Using set of 2.75mm double pointed needles and white wool pick up and knit 36(38,40) sts from st holder at back; 16 sts from st holder at top of sleeve; 44(48,52) sts from around front and 16 sts from st holder at top of sleeve. 112(118,124) sts. Work in single rib for 13cm. Cast off loosely in rib.

HEADBAND

Using 2.75mm needles and red yarn cast on 22(24,26) sts and work in single rib for 4cm.
Change to 3mm needles and work in pattern as for sweater until work meas 28(30,32)cm from beg. Change to size 2.75mm needles and work in single rib for 4cm. Cast off loosely in rib. Sew up both ends.

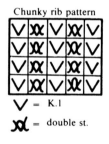

Chunky rib pattern

$\vee$ = K.1

$\bowtie$ = double st.

as seen from r.s. of work

BLOSSOM
Cardigan

Materials

Yarn: 25g balls 3 ply
Size: 9(12,18) mths
Instructions for 12mths and 18mths are in brackets. When only one number appears, it applies to all three sizes.
Quantity: 4(4,6)balls
One pair each 2.75mm and 3.25mm needles; 7 small white buttons.

Garment Measures

Chest	48	52	56	cm
Length	28	30	33	cm
Sleeve length	16	18	20	cm

TENSION
31 sts and 39 rows to 10cm in patt using 3.25mm needles.
IT IS IMPORTANT TO KNIT A TENSION SQUARE AND TO WORK TO STATED TENSION IN ORDER TO OBTAIN REQUIRED MEASUREMENTS. IF YOUR SQUARE IS BIGGER USE FINER NEEDLES. IF YOUR SQUARE IS SMALLER USE THICKER NEEDLES.

Stitches Used

1st and 2nd rows: k to end.
3rd row: * k1, p1 * rep from * to *.
4th row: knit all knit sts, purl all purl sts.

CARDIGAN

Back

Using 2.75mm needles cast on 74(80,86) sts and work in single rib for 4cm finishing with wsf. Change to 3.25mm needles and work patt as follows:
1st and 2nd rows: k to end.
3rd row: *k1,p1 * rep from * to *.
4th row: knit all knit sts, purl all purl sts.
These 4 rows form patt. Cont to work in patt until work meas 18(20,22)cm from beg.

Shape armholes
Cast off 6sts at beg of next 2 rows. 62(68,74) sts. Cont in patt until work meas 28(30,33)cm from beg.

Shape shoulders
Cast off 6(7,8) sts at beg of next 4 rows. Cast off centre 38(40,42) sts.

Left Front

Using 2.75mm needles, cast on 37(40,43) sts and work in single rib for 4cm finishing with wsf. Change to 3.25mm needles and work in patt as for back until work meas 18(20,22)cm from beg ending with rsf.

Shape armholes
Cast off 6sts at armhole edge, patt to end. 31(34,37) sts. Cont in patt until work meas 24(26,29)cm from beg ending with rsf.

Shape neck
Keeping patt correct, cast off at beg of next and each alt row 7(8,9) sts once, 4 sts once, 3 sts once, 2 sts once, 1 st 3 times. 12(14,16) sts. Cont in patt until work meas 28(30,33)cm from beg finishing with wsr.

Shape shoulder
At shoulder edge, cast off 6(7,8) sts at beg of next row, patt 1 row, cast off rem 6(7,8) sts.

Right Front

Work as for left front, reversing shapings. When working right front neck, end with wsf.

Sleeves
(both alike)

Using 2.75mm needles cast on 54(60,66) sts and work in single rib for 4cm. Change to 3.25mm needles and work in patt inc 1 st at both ends every 8(10,10) rows 5 times, 64(70,76) sts. Cont in patt until work meas 18(20,22)cm from beg. Cast off loosely.

Button Border

Using 2.75mm needles and with rsf pick up and knit 50(54,58) sts up side of left front. Work in single rib.
1st row: k3(4,5), (inc in next st) 44(46,48) times, k3(4,5). 94(100,106) sts *.

Cont in single rib for 7 more rows.
Next row: cast off in rib.

Buttonhole Border

Work as for button border to *. Cont in single rib for 2 rows ending with wsr.
Next row (buttonhole row): rib 4 sts, * yon, sl 1, k1, psso, rib 13(14,15) sts, rep from * 5 times more. Cont in single rib making 5 more buttonholes 13(14,15) sts apart. Cont in single rib for 4 rows.
Next row: cast off in rib.

To Make Up

Press each piece, except ribbing, with a warm iron and damp cloth. Do not overpress. Sew side seams. Sew shoulder seams.

Neckband

Using 2.75mm needles pick up and knit 72(80,88) sts around neck edge and work in single rib.
1st row: inc into 1st st and every alt st once. 108(120,132) sts. Cont in single rib for 2 rows.
Next row (buttonhole row): rib 5, y fwd, k2 tog, rib to end. Cont in single rib for 4 rows. Cast off in rib.

To Make Up

Sew sleeve seams leaving 2cm free at top. Sew in sleeves. Sew on buttons opposite buttonholes.

LOOK OF LACE
Jumper

To fit ages 2yrs, 4yrs, 6yrs

Materials

Cleckheaton 8 ply Machine Wash 50g balls
6 (7,8) balls
One pair each 4mm and 3.25mm
needles, 2 stitch holders, 3 buttons, cable
needle.

Measurements

Garment measures	67	72	77	cm
Back length	36	41	45	cm
Sleeve seam	21	25	31	cm

TENSION

22 sts to 10cm over st st, using 4mm
needles

**IT IS IMPORTANT TO KNIT A
TENSION SQUARE AND TO
WORK TO STATED TENSION IN
ORDER TO OBTAIN REQUIRED
MEASUREMENTS. IF YOUR
SQUARE IS BIGGER USE FINER
NEEDLES. IF YOUR SQUARE IS
SMALLER USE THICKER
NEEDLES.**

SPECIAL ABBREVIATIONS

"CR" = Slip next st onto a cable needle
and leave at back of work, k3, then k1
from cable needle.
"CL" = Slip next 3 sts onto cable needle
and leave at front of work, k1, then k3 from
cable needle.
"CRP" = Slip next st onto cable needle
and leave at back of work, k3, then p1
from cable needle.
"CLP" = Slip next 3 sts onto cable needle
and leave at front of work, p1, then k3
from cable needle.

Cable panel
(worked over 24 sts):
1st row: p8, "CR", "CL", p8.
2nd row: k8, p3, k2, p3, k8.
3rd row: p7, "CR", k2, "CL", p7.
4th row: k7, p3, k4, p3, k7.
5th row: p6, "CR", k4, "CL", p6.
6th row: k6, p3, k6, p3, k6.
7th row: p5, "CR", k6, "CL", p5.
8th row: k5, p3, k8, p3, k5.
9th row: p4, "CR", k8, "CL", p4.

10th row: k4, p3, k10, p3, k4.
11th row: p3, "CR", k10, "CL", p3.
12th row: k3, p3, k12, p3, k3.
13th row: p2, "CR", k12, "CL", p2.
14th row: k2, p3, k14, p3, k2.
15th row: p1, "CR", k14, "CL", p1.
16th row: k1, p3, k16, p3, k1.
17th row: p1, "CLP", k14, "CRP", p1.
18th row: as 14th row.
19th row: p2, "CLP", k12, "CRP", p2.
20th row: as 12th row.
21st row: p3, "CLP", k10, "CRP", p3.
22nd row: as 10th row.
23rd row: p4, "CLP", k8, "CRP", p4.
24th row: as 8th row.
25th row: p5, "CLP", k6, "CRP", p5.
26th row: as 6th row.
27th row: p6, "CLP", k4, "CRP", p6.
28th row: as 4th row.
29th row: p7, "CLP", k2, "CRP", p7.
30th row: as 2nd row.
31st row: p8, "CLP", "CRP", p8.
32nd row: k9, p0, k9.
Rows 1 to 32 inclusive form Cable Panel.

Lace Panel
(worked over 11 sts):
1st row: k3, k2tog, yfwd, k3, yfwd, sl 1, k1
psso, k1.
2nd and alt rows: purl.
3rd row: k2, k2tog, yfwd, k1, yfwd sl 1, k1,
psso, k2, yfwd, sl 1, k1, psso.
5th row: k1, k2tog, yfwd, k3, yfwd, sl 1,
k1, psso, k3.
7th row: k2tog, yfwd, k2, k2tog, yfwd, k1,
yfwd, sl 1, k1, psso, k2.
8th row: purl.
Rows 1 to 8 inclusive form Lace Panel.

Back

Using 3.25mm needles, cast on 70 (74,78)
sts.
1st row: k2, *p2, k2, rep from * to end.
2nd row: p2, *k2, p2, rep from * to end.
Repeat 1st and 2nd rows until band meas
4cm from beg, ending with a 1st row.
Next row: rib 9 (8.10), inc in next st, *rib
2, inc in next st. Rep from * to last 9 (8,10)
sts, rib 9 (8,10). 88 (94,98) sts.
Change to 4mm needles and beg patt.
1st row: p0 (0,1), k0 (1,2), p0 (2,2), * work
1st row of Lace Panel, p2, k2, p2, work 1st
row of Lace Panel *, p2, k2, work 1st row
of Cable Panel, k2, p2, rep from * to
once, p0 (2,2), k0 (1,2), p0 (0,1).
2nd row: k0 (0,1), p0 (1,2) k0 (2,2), *work
2nd row of Lace Panel, k2, p2, k2, work
2nd row of Lace Panel*, k2, p2, work 2nd
row of Cable Panel, p2, k2, rep from * to *
once, k0 (2,2), p0 (1,2), k0 (0,1).
3rd row: p0 (0,1), k0 (1,2), p0 (2,2), *work
3rd row of Lace Panel, p2, k2, p2, work
3rd row of Lace Panel*, p2, k2, work 3rd
row of Cable Panel, k2, p2, rep from * to
once, p0 (2,2), k0 (1,2), p0 (0,1).

Cont in patts as placed in last 3 rows until
work meas 35 (40,44)cm from beg, ending
with wsr.

Shape shoulders
Cast off 10 (11,11) sts at beg of next 4
rows, then 10 (10,12) sts at beg of foll 2
rows.
Leave rem 28 (30,30) sts on a stitch
holder.

Front

Work as for back until there are 16 (16,18)
rows less than back to shoulder shaping.

Shape neck
Next row: patt 37 (39,41), turn.
* * Dec one st at neck edge in every row
until 30 (32,34) sts rem.
Work 2 (2,4) rows. * *
Note: Left shoulder is shorter than right
shoulder to allow for button band.

Shape shoulder
Cast off 10 (11,11) sts at beg of next and
foll alt row.
Work 1 row. Cast off.
Slip next 14 (16,16) sts on a stitch holder.
Join yarn to rem sts and patt to end.
Rep from * * to * *
Work 7 rows.

Shape shoulder
Complete as for other shoulder.

Sleeves

Using 3.25mm needles, cast on 38 (42,46)
sts.
Cont in rib as for lower band of back until
band meas 3cm from beg, ending with a
2nd row and inc 15 (15,11) sts evenly
across last row. 53 (57,57) sts.
Change to 4mm needles.
1st row: p0 (2,2), *k2, p2, k3, k2tog, yfwd,
k3, yfwd, sl 1, k1, psso, k1, p2, rep from *
to last 2 (4,4) sts, k2, p0 (2,2).
2nd and alt rows: k0 (2,2), *p2, k2, p11,
k2, rep from * to last 2 (4,4) sts, p2, k0
(2,2).
3rd row: p0 (2,2), *k2, p2, k2, k2tog, yfwd,
k1, yfwd, sl 1, k1, psso, k2, yfwd, sl 1, k1,
psso, p2, rep from * to last 2 (4,4) sts, k2,
p0 (2,2).
5th row: p0 (2,2), *k2, p2, k1, k2tog, yfwd,
k3, yfwd, sl 1, k1, psso, k3, p2, rep from *
to last 2 (4,4) sts, k2, p0 (2,2).
7th row: p0 (2,2), *k2, p2, k2tog, yfwd, k2,
k2tog, yfwd, k1, yfwd, sl 1, k1, psso, k2,
p2, rep from * to last 2 (4,4) sts, k2, p0
(2,2).
8th row: as 2nd row.
Rows 1 to 8 inclusive form patt.
Cont in patt inc one st at each end of next

and foll 6th (8th,4th) rows until there are 63 (65,69) sts, then in foll 8th (10th,6th) row/s until there are 65 (69,83) sts (noting to work extra sts into patt).
Cont without shaping until side edge meas 21 (25,31)cm from beg, working last row on wrong side.

Shape top

Cast off 8 (9,11) sts at beg of next 4 rows, then 9 (9,12) sts at beg of foll 2 rows.
Cast off rem sts.

Neckband

Using back stitch, join right shoulder seam. With rsf using 3.25mm needles, beg at left shoulder, knit up 74 (78,82) sts evenly along neck edge (including sts from stitch holders).
Cont in rib as for lower band of back (beg with a 2nd row) until work measures 2cm from beg, ending with a 2nd row.
Cast off loosely in rib.

Left Front Shoulder Band

With right side facing, using 3.25mm needles, knit up 30 (34,38) sts evenly along left front edge and side of neckband.
Work 1 row rib as for lower band of back (beg with a 2nd row).
Next row: rib 6, cast on 2 sts, [rib 8 (10,12), cast on 2 sts] twice, rib 2.
Next row: rib 2, cast on 2 sts, [rib 8 (10,12), cast on 2 sts] twice, rib 6.
Work 2 rows rib.
Cast off loosely in rib.

Right Back Shoulder Band

With rsf, using 3.25mm needles, knit up 30 (34,38) sts evenly along right back edge and side of neckband.
Work 5 rows rib as for lower band of back (beg with a 2nd row).
Cast off loosely in rib.

To Make Up

Overlap shoulder band at armhole edge, and stitch in position. Sew in sleeves placing centre of sleeves to shoulder seams. Join side and sleeve seams.

BUNNY HOP
Jumper

To fit ages 2yrs, 4yrs, 6yrs

Materials

Cleckheaton 8 ply Machine Wash 50g balls 6 (7,8) balls
One pair each 4mm and 3.25mm and 1 set of 3.25mm needles, cable needle, 2 stitch holders, 3 buttons.

Measurements

Garment measures	63	68	73	cm
Back length	36	40	44	cm
Sleeve seam	23	28	33	cm

TENSION
21 sts to 10cm over moss st, using 4mm needles and 22 sts to 10cm over st st, using 4mm needles.
IT IS IMPORTANT TO KNIT A TENSION SQUARE AND TO WORK TO STATED TENSION IN ORDER TO OBTAIN REQUIRED MEASUREMENTS. IF YOUR SQUARE IS BIGGER USE FINER NEEDLES. IF YOUR SQUARE IS SMALLER USE THICKER NEEDLES.

SPECIAL ABBREVIATIONS

"C4F" = Slip next 2 sts onto cable needle and leave at front of work, k2, then k2 from cable needle.
"C4B" = Slip next 2 sts onto cable needle and leave at back of work, k2, then k2 from cable needle.
"T4B" = Slip next 2 sts onto cable needle and leave at back of work, k2, then p2 from cable needle.
"T4F" = Slip next 2 sts onto cable needle and leave at front of work, p2, then k2 from cable needle.
"BC" = Slip next st onto cable needle and leave at back of work, k1tbl, then p1 from cable needle.
"FC" = Slip next st onto cable needle and leave at front of work, p1, then k1tbl from cable needle.
"TW" = Knit into front of second st on left hand needle, then into front of first st, slipping both sts off needle tog.

Patt Panel A
(worked over 9 sts):
1st row: p3, k3tbl, p3.
2nd row: k3, p3tbl, k3.
3rd row: p2, "BC", k1tbl, "FC", p2.
4th row: k2, (p1tbl, k1) twice, p1tbl, k2.
5th row: p1, "BC", p1, k1tbl, p1, "FC", p1.
6th row: k1, (p1tbl, k2) twice, p1tbl, k1.
7th row: "BC", p1, k3tbl, p1, "FC".
8th row: p1tbl, k2, p3tbl, k2, p1tbl.
Rows 1 to 8 inclusive form Patt Panel A.

Patt Panel B
(worked over 16 sts):
1st row: k2, p4, "C4B", p4, k2.
2nd row: p2, k4, p1, k4, p2.
3rd row: k2, p4, k4, p4, k2.
4th row: as 2nd row.
5th row: ("T4F", "T4B") twice.
6th row: as 3rd row.
7th row: as 2nd row.
8th row: as 3rd row.
9th row: p2, "C4B", p4, "C4B", p2.
10th row: as 3rd row.
11th row: as 9th row.
12th row: as 3rd row.
13th row: as 2nd row.
14th row: as 3rd row.
15th row: ("T4B", "T4F") twice.
16th row: as 2nd row.
17th row: as 3rd row.
18th row: as 2nd row.
19th row: as 1st row.
20th row: as 2nd row.
Rows 1 to 20 inclusive form Patt Panel B.

Patt Panel C
(worked over 12 sts):
1st row: "TW", p2, "C4F", p2, "TW".
2nd row: p2, k2, p4, k2, p2.
3rd row: "TW", p2, k4, p2, "TW".
4th row: as 2nd row.
Rows 1 to 4 inclusive form Patt Panel C.

Patt Panel D
(worked over 12 sts):
Work as for Patt Panel C, noting to work "C4B" in place of "C4F".

Back

Using 3.25mm needles, cast on 71 (75, 81) sts.
1st row: k2, *p1, k1, rep from * to last st, k1.
2nd row: k1, *p1, k1, rep from * to end.
Repeat 1st and 2nd rows until band meas 4 (4,5)cm from beg, ending with a 1st row.
Next row: rib 9 (11,13), (inc in next st, rib 1) 27 times, rib 8 (10,14). 98 (102,108) sts.
Change to 4mm needles.
1st row: p0 (0,1), (K1,p1) 2 (3,4) times, p2, *work 1st row of Patt Panel C across next 12 sts, work 1st row of Patt Panel A

across next 9 sts, work 1st row of Patt Panel D across next 12 sts*, p2, work 1st row of Patt Panel B across next 16 sts, p2, rep from * to *, p2, (p1,k1) 2 (3,4) times, p0 (0,1).

2nd row: k0 (0,1), (p1,k1) 2 (3,4) times, k2, *work 2nd row of Patt Panel D across next 12 sts, work 2nd row of Patt Panel A across next 9 sts, work 2nd row of Patt Panel C across next 12 sts*, k2, work 2nd row of Patt Panel B across next 16 sts, k2, rep from * to *, k2, (k1,p1) 2 (3,4) times, k0 (0,1).

3rd row: k0 (0,1), (p1,k1) 2 (3,4) times, p2, *work 3rd row of Patt Panel C across next 12 sts, work 3rd row of Patt Panel A across next 9 sts, work 3rd row of Patt Panel D across next 12 sts*, p2, work 3rd row of Patt Panel B across next 16 sts, p2, rep from * to *, p2, (k1,p1) 2 (3,4) times, k0 (0,1).

4th row: p0 (0,1), (k1,p1) 2 (3,4) times, k2, *work 4th row of Patt Panel D across next 12 sts, work 4th row of Patt Panel A across next 9 sts, work 4th row of Patt Panel C across next 12 sts*, k2, work 4th row of Patt Panel B across next 16 sts, k2, rep from * to *, k2, (p1,k1) 2 (3,4) times, p0 (0,1).

Keeping moss st sides and all patts correct as placed in last 4 rows, cont in patt until work meas 35 (39,43)cm from beg, working last row on wrong side.

Shape shoulders
Keeping patts correct, cast off 9 (9,10) sts at beg of next 6 rows, then 9 (10,9) sts at beg of foll 2 rows.
Leave rem 26 (28,30) sts on a stitch holder.

Front

Work as given for back, until there are 18 (20,22) rows less than back to shoulder shaping.

Shape neck
1st row: patt 42 (44,47), turn.
**Keeping patts correct, dec one st at neck edge in alt rows until 36 (37,39) sts rem.
Work 5 rows**.

Shape shoulder
Keeping patts correct, cast off 9 (9,10) sts at beg of next and alt rows 3 times in all.
Work 1 row. Cast off rem sts.
Slip next 14 sts onto stitch holder and leave. Join yarn to rem sts and patt to end.
Work as given from ** to **.
Work 1 row.

Shape shoulder
Complete as for other shoulder.

Sleeves

Using 3.25mm needles, cast on 37 (37,39) sts.
Work in rib as given for lower band of back, until band meas 4cm from beg, ending with a 1st row.
Next row: rib 6 (6,8), inc in each of next 25 (25,23) sts, rib 6 (6,8). 62 sts.
Change to 4mm needles.
1st row: Work 1st row of Patt Panel A across next 9 sts, work 1st row of Patt Panel D across next 12 sts, p2, work 1st row of Patt Panel B across next 16 sts, p2, work 1st row of Patt Panel C across next 12 sts, work 1st row of Patt Panel A across next 9 sts.
Cont in patts as placed in last row, inc one st at each end of foll 4th rows until there are 68 (72,76) sts, then in foll 6th rows until there are 78 (84,90) sts, working extra sts into patt panels as for back.
Cont in patts until side edge meas 23 (28,33)cm from beg, working last row on wrong side.

Shape top
Keeping patts correct, cast off 7 sts at beg of next 8 rows.
Cast off rem sts.

Neckband

Using back stitch, join shoulder seams. With right side facing, using set of 3.25mm needles, beg at left shoulder seam, knit up 76 (82,90) sts evenly round neck edge (including sts from stitch holders).
1st round: *k1, p1, rep from * to end.
Repeat 1st round until neckband meas 3cm from beg.
Cast off loosely in rib.

To Make Up

Using back stitch, sew in sleeves placing centre of sleeve to shoulder seams. Join side and sleeve seams. Sew on buttons for decoration.

TOMBOY
Jumper

To fit ages 3yrs, 5yrs, 7yrs

Materials

Yarn: 8 ply 100g balls
Approx. 1 ball each of 4 colours:
Green fleck, Green, Red fleck and Red.
One pair each 3.5mm and 4.5mm
needles, stitch holder, 4 buttons.

> **TENSION**
> 18 sts and 25 rows to 10 cm over
> st st using 4.5mm needles.
> **IT IS IMPORTANT TO KNIT A
> TENSION SQUARE AND TO
> WORK TO STATED TENSION IN
> ORDER TO OBTAIN REQUIRED
> MEASUREMENTS. IF YOUR
> SQUARE IS BIGGER USE FINER
> NEEDLES. IF YOUR SQUARE IS
> SMALLER USE THICKER
> NEEDLES.**

Front/Back

Jumper is knitted in one piece beginning
with the Front.
Using 3.5mm needles and green flecked
yarn cast on 59 (63, 67) sts and work in
single (k1, p1) for 5 cm. Change to
4.5mm needles and st st increasing 8 sts
evenly across the 1st row. Cont in st st
until work meas 31 (34, 37) cm.
Next row: k27 (30, 32), cast off next 13
(14, 15) sts, change to red yarn and k to
end.
Next row: p to last 3 sts, p3 tog.
Next row: knit.
Next row: purl to last 3 sts, p3 tog.
Next row: knit.
Next row: purl to last 2 sts, p2 tog.
22 (24,26) sts.
Work until there are 15 rows in red.
Tie a coloured marker at each end of next
row to indicate shoulder line. Cont until
there are 20 rows red, casting on 2 sts at
neck edge on 17th and 19th rows. 26
(28,30) sts.
Knit 1 row. Slip sts onto a st holder.
Join green yarn to left shoulder and work
to correspond with right side, shaping in
reverse.
Work 9 rows green.
Next row: cast off all sts to form button
placket.
Using 4.5mm needles and green yarn
cast on 22 (24,26) sts.
1st row: purl.
Cont in st st casting on 2 sts at the neck

edge in 9th and 11th rows.
12th row: purl 26 (28,30) sts.
13th row: change to red flecked yarn,
k26 (28,30), cast on 15 sts for back neck,
knit across sts on st holder. 67 (72,77)
sts.
Cont working on these sts in st st until
work meas 69 (75,81) cm ending with a
k row.
Next row: dec 8 sts evenly across row.
Change to 3.5mm needles and work in
single rib for 5 cm. Cast off.

Left Sleeve

Using 3.5mm needles and red flecked
yarn cast on 34 (36,38) sts and work in
single rib for 4 cm.
Change to 4.5mm needles, green yarn
and st st, working as follows: k2, inc in
next st, work to last 3 sts, inc in next st,
k2.
Inc as above in every 6th row 9 (10,11)
times. 58 (62,66) sts.
Cont until work meas 26 (29,32) cm. Cast
off.

Right Sleeve

Work as for left sleeve using green
flecked yarn instead of red flecked yarn
and red yarn instead of green.

Neckband

Using 3.5mm needles and green yarn
pick up 4 sts every 5 rows, every cast off
st and 1 st every purl row around neck
edge.
Work 3 cm in single rib. Cast off loosely
in rib.

Shoulder Fastening

Using 3.5mm needles and green yarn
pick up 6 sts from neckband end and 25
(27,29) sts evenly along shoulder edge of
back. 31 (33, 35) sts.
Work 2 rows single rib.
Next row (buttonhole row): rib 5, cast off
2 sts, rib 5, cast off 2 sts, rib 5, cast off
2 sts, rib 5, cast off 2 sts, rib to end.
Next row: Work in rib casting on 2 sts
over cast off sts in previous row.

Cont in single rib for 4 rows. Cast off
loosely in rib.

To Make Up

Lap left back shoulder opening over front.
Slipstitch into place. Sew sleeves into
armholes, placing centre sleeve top at
marker. Sew side and sleeve seams. Sew
on buttons.

Picture Book Knits

No child could resist a birthday jumper
adorned with Australia's favourite characters,
Blinky Bill or Nutsy. There are more animal friends
on Kitty and Tom and Zoo Friends. For fantasy fun,
Chopper Pilots and Firefighter will complete the
picture. Satisfy their sweet tooth with Lolly Pop,
or complement those early spring days with her
very own rose garden.

BLINKY BILL
Jumper

Materials

Cleckheaton 8ply Pure Wool 50g balls
Main Colour (MC-Cream)   6 (7,8) balls
1 ball each of 7 colours:
(C1-Brown), (C3-Mustard),
(C4-Dark Grey), (C5-Grey),
(C7-White) and (C8-Dark Brown)
Cleckheaton 8ply Machine Wash 50g balls
2nd Contrast (C2-Red)   1 ball
1 pair each 4mm, 3.25mm and one set of
3.25mm needles, 2 stitch holders,
bobbins, tapestry needle for embroidery.

Measurements

To fit underarm	61	66	71	cm
Actual measurement	71	76	81	cm
Length to back				
neck (approx)	41	44	48	cm
Sleeve seam	26	31	36	cm

TENSION
22 sts to 10cm over st st on 4mm
needles.
**IT IS IMPORTANT TO KNIT A
TENSION SQUARE AND TO
WORK TO STATED TENSION IN
ORDER TO OBTAIN REQUIRED
MEASUREMENTS. IF YOUR
SQUARE IS BIGGER USE FINER
NEEDLES. IF YOUR SQUARE IS
SMALLER USE THICKER
NEEDLES.**

Front

Using 3.25mm needles and MC, cast on
71 (75,81) sts.
1st row: k2, * p1, k1, rep from * to last st,
k1.
2nd row: k1, * p1, k1, rep from * to end.
Rep 1st and 2nd rows until band
measures 4 (5,5) cm from beg, ending
with a 2nd row and inc 10sts evenly
across last row. 81 (85,91) sts.
Change to 4mm needles. * * *
Using MC, work 0 (2,6) rows st st (1 row k,
1 row p).

NOTE: When changing colours in centre
of row, twist the colour to be used
underneath and to the right of colour just
used, making sure both yarns are worked
firmly at joins. Always change colours on
wrong side of work so colour change does
not show on right side. Use a separate ball
of yarn for each section of colour. We
suggest using bobbins. Wind a quantity of
yarn around bobbin and place end
through slot to hold. Unwind only enough
yarn to knit required sts, then place yarn in
slot, keeping bobbin close to work.
Work rows 1 to 88 inclusive from Graph.
Using MC, work 2 (6,12) rows.

Shape neck
Next row: k34 (36,39), turn.
* * Dec one st at neck edge in foll alt rows
5 (6,6) times. 29 (30,33) sts.
Work 11 (11,13) rows. * *

Shape shoulder
Cast off 10 (10,11) sts at beg of next row
and foll alt row.
Work 1 row. Cast off.
Slip next 13 sts onto a stitch holder and
leave.
With right side facing, join yarn to rem sts
and knit to end.
Rep from * * to * *.
Work 1 row.

Shape shoulder
Complete as for other shoulder.

Back

Work as for Front to * * *.
Using MC only, cont in st st until work
measures same as Front to shoulder
shaping.

Shape shoulders
Cast off 10 (10,11) sts at beg of next 4
rows, then 9 (10,11) sts at beg of foll 2
rows.
Leave rem 23 (25,25) sts on a stitch
holder.

Sleeves

Using 3.25mm needles and MC, cast on
39 (41,43) sts.
Work for 4 (5,5)cm in rib as for lower band
of Back, ending with a 2nd row and inc 12
sts evenly across last row. 51 (53,55) sts.
Change to 4mm needles.
Cont in st st, inc one st at each end of 3rd
row, then in foll 6th rows until there are 61
(67,77) sts, then in foll 8th rows until there
are 67 (73,81) sts.
Cont without shaping until side edge
measures 26 (31,36)cm from beg, ending
with a purl row.

Shape top
Cast off 8 (9,10) sts at beg of next 6 rows.
Cast off rem sts.

Neckband

Using back stitch, join shoulder seams.
With right side facing, using set of 3.25mm
needles, beg at left shoulder seam, knit up
80 (84,86) sts evenly around neck edge
(Including sts from stitch holders).
1st round: *k1, p1, rep from * to end.
Rep 1st round until neckband measures
5cm from beg.
Cast off loosely in rib.

To Make Up

Using stem stitch and C6 (noting to splice
yarn to $\frac{2}{3}$ thickness), embroider outlines
and features on Blinky Bill, using diagram
as a guide. Using back stitch, sew in
sleeves placing centre of sleeves to
shoulder seams. Join side and sleeve
seams.
Fold neckband in half onto wrong side and
loosely slip st in position.

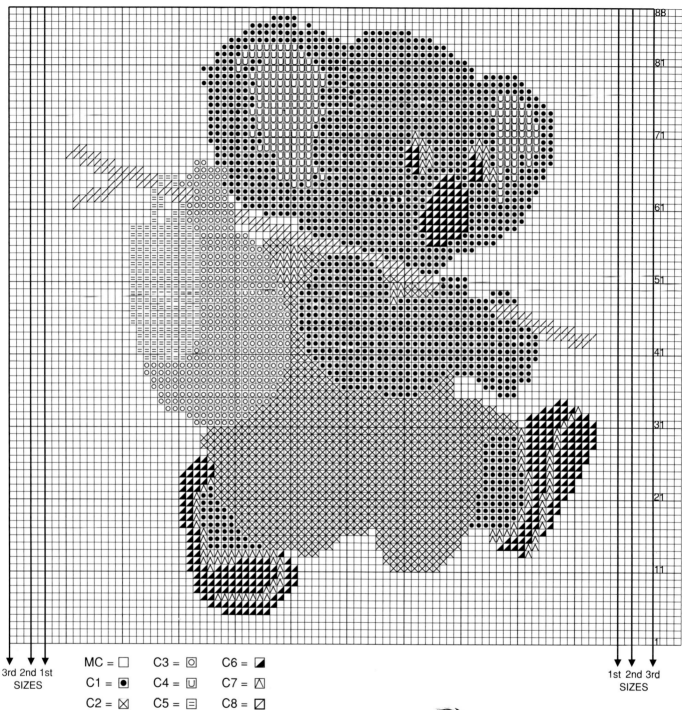

3rd 2nd 1st
SIZES

1st 2nd 3rd
SIZES

MC = ☐   C3 = ⊙   C6 = ◢
C1 = ⊡   C4 = Ⓤ   C7 = ◁
C2 = ⊠   C5 = ⊟   C8 = ▨

Note: When working from graph work
all odd numbered rows (knit rows) from
right to left, and all even numbered
rows (purl rows) from left to right.
Each square represents a stitch.

NUTSY
Jumper

Measurements

To fit underarm	61	66	71	cm
Actual measurement	71	76	81	cm
Length to back				
neck (approx)	41	45	49	cm
Sleeve seam	26	31	36	cm

Materials

Cleckheaton 8 ply Machine Wash 50g balls
Main Colour (MC-Cream)   7 (8,9) balls
C4 (Green)   1 ball
Cleckheaton 8ply Pure Wool (50g) balls
1 ball each of 6 colours:
(C1-Brown), (C2-Yellow),
(C3-Red), (C5-Grey),
(C6-Black) and (C7-White)
1 pr each 4mm, 3.25mm and 1 set of
3.25mm knitting needles, 2 stitch holders,
bobbins, tapestry needle for embroidery.

TENSION

22 sts to 10cm over st st on 4mm
needles.
**IT IS IMPORTANT TO KNIT A
TENSION SQUARE AND TO
WORK TO STATED TENSION IN
ORDER TO OBTAIN REQUIRED
MEASUREMENTS. IF YOUR
SQUARE IS BIGGER USE FINER
NEEDLES. IF YOUR SQUARE IS
SMALLER USE THICKER
NEEDLES.**

Front

Using 3.25mm needles and MC, cast on
71 (75,81) sts.
1st row: k2, *p1, k1, rep from * to last st,
k1.
2nd row: k1, *p1, k1, rep from * to end.
Rep 1st and 2nd rows until band
measures 4 (5,5) cm from beg, ending
with a 2nd row and inc 10 sts evenly
across last row. 81 (85,91) sts.
Change to 4 mm needles. * * *
Using MC, work 0 (2,6) rows st st (1 row k,
1 row p).
NOTE: When changing colours in centre
of row, twist the colour to be used

underneath and to the right of colour just
used, making sure both yarns are worked
firmly at joins. Always change colours on
wrong side of work so colour change does
not show on right side. Use a separate
ball of yarn for each section of colour. We
suggest using bobbins. Wind a quantity of
yarn around bobbin and place end
through slot to hold. Unwind only enough
yarn to knit required sts, then place yarn in
slot, keeping bobbin close to work.
Work rows 1 to 88 inclusive from Graph.
Using MC, work 2 (6,12) rows.

Shape neck
Next row: k34 (36,39), turn.
* * Dec one st at neck edge in foll alt rows
5 (6,6) times, 29 (30,33) sts.
Work 11 (11,13) rows. * *

Shape shoulder
Cast off 10 (10,11) sts at beg of next row
and foll alt row.
Work 1 row. Cast off.
Slip next 13 sts onto a stitch holder and
leave. With right side facing, join yarn to
rem sts and knit to end.
Rep from * * to * *
Work 1 row.

Shape shoulder
Complete as for other shoulder.

Back

Work as for Front to * * *. Using MC only,
cont in st st until work measures same as
front to shoulder shaping.

Shape Shoulders
Cast off 10 (10,11) sts at beg of next 4
rows, then 9 (10,11) sts at beg of foll 2
rows. Leave rem 23 (25,25) sts on a stitch
holder.

Sleeves

Using 3.25mm needles and MC, cast on
39 (41,43) sts. Work for 4 (5,5)cm in rib as
for lower band of Back, ending with a 2nd
row and inc 12 sts evenly across last row.
51 (53,55) sts. Change to 4mm needles.
Cont in st st, inc one st at each end of 3rd
row, then in foll 6th rows until there are 61
(67,77) sts, then in foll 8th rows until there
are 67 (73,81) sts. Cont without shaping
until side edge measures 26 (31,36)cm
from beg ending with a purl row.

Shape top
Cast off 8 (9,10) sts at beg of next 6 rows.
Cast off rem sts.

Neckband

Using back stitch, join shoulder seams.
With right side facing, using set of 3.25mm
needles, and MC, beg at left shoulder
seam, knit up 80 (84,86) sts evenly around
neck edge (including sts from stitch
holders).
1st round: * k1, p1, rep from * to end. Rep
1st round until neckband measures 5 cm
from beg. Cast off loosely in rib.

To Make Up

Slice yarn to $\frac{2}{3}$ thickness. Using stem stitch
and C6, embroider outlines and features
on Nutsy, using diagram as a guide. Using
C2 embroider lazy daisy flowers in her
hand, then using C6 and stem stitch,
embroider stems of flowers as illustrated.
Using C3 and knitting stitch embroider
spots on dress as illustrated. Using back
stitch, sew in sleeves placing centre of
sleeves to shoulder seams. Join side and
sleeve seams. Fold neck band in half onto
wrong side and **loosely** slip st in position.

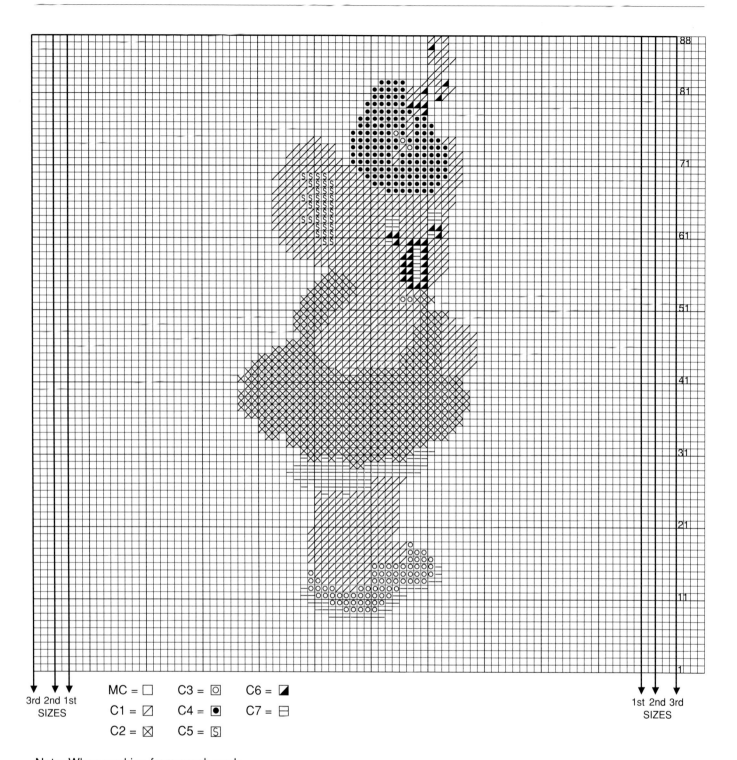

3rd 2nd 1st
SIZES

MC = □   C3 = ◉   C6 = ◪

C1 = ▨   C4 = ◉   C7 = ⊟

C2 = ⊠   C5 = ⑤

1st 2nd 3rd
SIZES

Note: When working from graph work
all odd numbered rows (knit rows) from
right to left, and all even numbered
rows (purl rows) from left to right.
Each square represents a stitch.

ROSIE
Cardigan

To fit ages 4yrs, 6yrs, 8yrs

Materials

Cleckheaton 8 ply Pure Wool 50g balls
Main colour (MC)   6 (7,8) balls
1 ball each of 2 contrast
colours (C1 and C2)
One pair each 4mm and 3.25mm needles,
3 stitch holders, 7 buttons, tapestry needle
for embroidery.

Measurements

Garment measures	69	76	83	cm
Back length	38	42	46	cm
Sleeve seam	27	32	36	cm

TENSION
22 sts to 10cm over st st on 4mm
needles.
**IT IS IMPORTANT TO KNIT A
TENSION SQUARE AND TO
WORK TO STATED TENSION IN
ORDER TO OBTAIN REQUIRED
MEASUREMENTS. IF YOUR
SQUARE IS BIGGER USE FINER
NEEDLES. IF YOUR SQUARE IS
SMALLER USE THICKER
NEEDLES.**

Back

Using 3.25mm needles and MC, cast on
77 (85,93) sts.
1st row: k2, *p1, k1, rep from * to last st,
k1.
2nd row: k1, *p1, k1, rep from * to end.
Rep 1st and 2nd rows until work meas 5
(5,6) cm from beg, ending with a 2nd row.
Change to 4mm needles.
Cont in st st until work meas 24
(26,28)cm from beg, ending with a purl
row.

Shape raglan armholes
Cast off 2 sts at beg of next 2 rows.
3rd row: k1, sl 1, k1, psso, knit to last 3
sts, k2tog, k1.
4th row: purl.
Rep 3rd and 4th rows 14 (16,19) times,
then 3rd row once. 41 (45,47) sts.
Next row: p1, p2tog, purl to last 3 sts,
p2togtbl, p1.

Rep last 2 rows until 23 (23,25) sts rem.
Leave rem sts on a stitch holder.

Left Front

Using 3.25mm needles and MC, cast on
39 (43,47) sts.
Work in rib as for lower band of Back until
work meas 5 (5,6) cm from beg, ending
with a 2nd row.
Change to 4mm needles.
Cont in st st until work meas 24
(26,28) cm from beg, ending with a purl
row.

Shape raglan armhole
Cast off 2 sts at beg of next row.
Work 1 row.
3rd row: k1, sl 1, k1, psso, knit to end.
4th row: purl.
Rep 3rd and 4th rows 11 (13,16) times,
then 3rd row once. 24 (26,27) sts.

Shape neck
Next row: cast off 5 (5,6) sts, purl to end.
Dec one st at armhole edge (as before) in
next and foll alt rows 3 times in all, then
in every row 8 (10,10) times, AT SAME
TIME dec one st at neck edge in next and
foll alt rows 5 times in all. 3 sts.
Next row: p2tog, p1.
Next row: sl 1, k1, psso. Fasten off.

Right Front

Work to correspond with Left Front,
noting to begin raglan and neck shaping
one row higher, and to work raglan
shaping as for right edge of Back.

Sleeves

Using 3.25mm needles and MC, cast on
35 (35,37) sts.
Work in rib as for lower band of Back,
until band meas 5 (5,6) cm from beg,
ending with a 2nd row and inc 4 (6,6) sts
evenly across last row. 39 (41,43) sts.
Change to 4mm needles.
Cont in st st, inc one st at each end of 5th
row and foll 8th (10th,10th) rows until
there are 51 (55,59) sts.
Cont without shaping until side edge
meas 27 (32,36) cm from beg, ending
with a purl row.

Shape raglan
Cast off 2 sts at beg of next 2 rows.
3rd row: k1, sl 1, k1, psso, knit to last 3
sts, k2tog, k1.
4th row: purl.
Work 0 (2,2) rows st st. 45 (49,53) sts.
3RD SIZE ONLY:
Rep last 4 rows once. 51 sts.

ALL SIZES:
Rep 3rd and 4th rows 19 (21,22) times. 7
sts.
Leave rem sts on a stitch holder.

Right Front Band

Using 3.25mm needles and MC, cast on
7 sts.
Work 5 rows garter st (every row knit —
1st row is wrong side).
6th row: k3, yfwd, k2tog, k2.
Work 21 (23,25) rows g st.
Rep last 22 (24,26) rows 4 times, then
first 18 (20,22) of these 22 (24,26) rows
once.
DO NOT BREAK OFF YARN. Leave sts
on a spare needle.

Left Front Band

Work as for Right Front Band, omitting
buttonholes, working one row less, and
breaking off yarn.

Neckband

Using back stitch, join raglan seams,
noting that tops of sleeves form part of
neckline. With rsf, using 3.25mm needles
and MC, holding Right Front Band sts,
knit up 77 (81,83) sts evenly around neck
edge, including sts from stitch holders,
then knit across Left Front Band sts. 91
(95,97) sts. Work 3 rows g st.
4th row: k3, yfwd, k2tog, k2.
Work 5 rows g st.
Cast off.

To Make Up

Using backstitch, join side and sleeve
seams. Sew Front Bands in position.
Using C1 and C2 and Knitting Stitch,
embroider flowers at random as
illustrated. Sew on buttons.

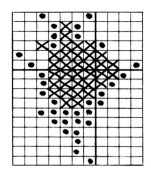

	MC		C1		C2

LOLLY POP
Jumper

To fit ages 4yrs, 6yrs, 8yrs

Materials

Mohair or Brushed Wool 50g balls 8 ply
Main Colour (MC)
(white)   4 balls
1 ball each of C1 (red);
C2 (blue); C3 (apricot);
C4 (beige); C5 (hot
pink); C6 (pink); C7
(yellow); and C8 (grey).
One pair each 3mm and 3.75mm
needles; stitch holders; 4 buttons.

Measurements

Garment measures	64	68	72 cm
Back length	35	38	40 cm
Sleeve seam	26	27.5	29 cm

TENSION

22 sts and 30 rows to 10 cm over
st st on 3.75mm needles.
**IT IS IMPORTANT TO KNIT A
TENSION SQUARE AND TO
WORK TO STATED TENSION IN
ORDER TO OBTAIN REQUIRED
MEASUREMENTS. IF YOUR
SQUARE IS BIGGER USE FINER
NEEDLES. IF YOUR SQUARE IS
SMALLER USE THICKER
NEEDLES.**

Back

Using 3mm needles and C1, cast on 60
(62,66) sts.
Rib k1 p1 for 4 cm, inc 13 (15,15) sts
evenly along last row to 73 (77,81) sts.
Break off C1. *
Using 3.75mm needles, MC and st st
cont until work meas 25.5 (28.5,30.5) cm
from beg, ending with wsr.

Shape neck
k23 (25,27) sts, turn. On these sts only
cast off 4 sts, 2 sts and 1 st at neck edge
on next and foll 2 alt rows. 16 (18,20) sts.
Cont straight until work meas 32
(35,37) cm from beg, ending with wsr.
Break off MC. Place sts on holder.
Return to rem sts. Place centre 27 sts
onto holder.

Working with more than one
colour adds a new dimension to
your knitting. The simplest of
these is a horizontal stripe
pattern in two or more colours.
The different yarns should be
changed over at the right hand
edge. Providing the stripes are
narrow and only 2 or 3 colours
are being used the yarns can be
carried up the right hand side of
the work without having to break
off and rejoin a colour every time
it is needed.
    Where 2 colours are used
repeatedly in the same row but
not more than 5 stitches apart
the best way to carry the
different yarns is by stranding.
This involves carrying the yarns
loosely at the back of the work.
Where the yarn needs to be
carried over more than 5 stitches
or if there are 3 or more colours
it is best to use the weaving
method where the yarn not being
used is woven through the back
of the work.
    For changing colours when
knitting large blocks of colour,
such as in picture knitting, the
yarns must be twisted quite
tightly at the back of the work at
each colour change. This is the
intarsia method and depends on
this twisting to ensure that there
are no holes at the joins. When
the piece is complete loose ends
are darned in on the wrong side.
    Where a number of colours are
being used in a single row it is best
to invest in some knitting bobbins.
These are quite inexpensive plastic
holders which keep the various
strands of yarn from tangling
together as you work.

Rejoin yarn at neck edge, work 2nd half
to match, shaping in reverse.
Break off MC.
With rsf and C1, rib k1 p1 16 (18,20) sts
from holder, pick up and k7 sts down
right neck, rib sts on centre holder, dec 1
st in centre [26 sts], pick up and k7 sts up
left neck, rib sts on holder. 72 (76,80)
sts. ** Rib for 3 cm, ending with wsr.
Next row: rib 23 (25,27) sts, cast off 26
sts, rib to end.
Work 1 row. Keeping rib correct, cast off
4 sts, 2 sts and 1 st at neck edge on next
and foll 2 alt rows. Cont in rib until work
meas 38 (41,43) cm from beg, ending
with wsr. Cast off in rib.
Return to rem sts. Rejoin yarn at neck
edge and cast off 4 sts. Work 2nd half to
match, shaping in reverse.

Front

Cast on and work as for Back to *
Using 3.75mm needles and MC, st st for
3 rows.
Beg chart as follows, working chart from
right to left on k rows and left to right on
p rows. Carry yarn across back of work,
taking care to keep tension even — if
taking yarn across more than 8 sts, use
separate ball of C, twisting yarns to link
sts.
4th row: p43 (45,47) MC, p3 C1, p6 MC,
p2 C6, MC to end.
5th row: k18 (20,22) MC, k4 C6, k4 MC,
k5 C1, MC to end.
Work 62 rows from chart as set. Break off
MC, join C8 as MC.

When chart has been completed, cont in
C8 only until work meas 25.5
(28.5,30.5) cm from beg, ending with
wsr.

Shape neck
Work as for Back to **
Rib for 1.5 cm.
Next row: rib 5 (6,7), cast off 2 sts, rib 6,
cast off 2 sts, rib 42 (44,46) sts, cast off
2 sts, rib 6, cast off 2 sts, rib to end.
Next row: work in rib, casting on 2 sts
over cast-off sts on previous row.
Work in rib until work meas 35 (38,40) cm
from beg, ending with wsr. Cast off all sts
in rib.

Sleeves

Using 3mm needles and C1, cast on 36
(40,44) sts.
Rib k1 p1 for 3 cm, inc 6 sts evenly along
last row to 42 (46,50) sts.
Break off C1.
Using 3.75mm needles, MC and st st,
beg to work from Chart B, inc 1 st each
end of 3rd and every foll 4th row to 72
(76,80) sts.
Cont straight until sleeve meas 26
(27.5,29) cm from beg, ending with wsr.
Cast off loosely.

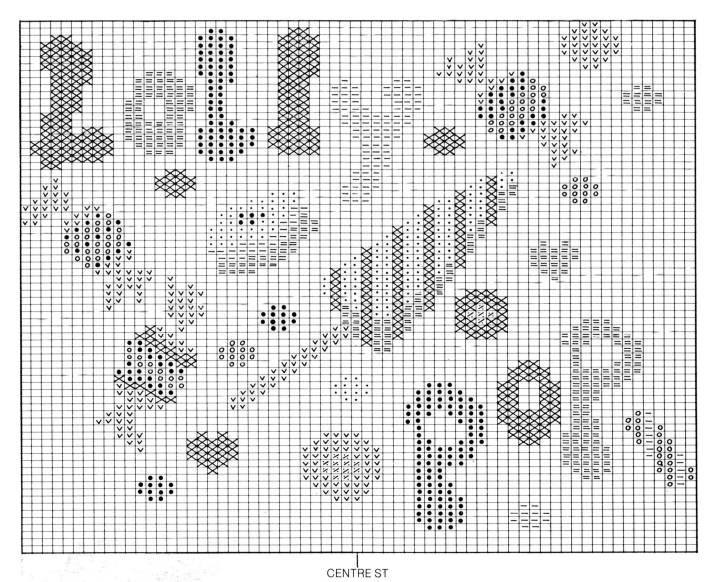

CENTRE ST

GRAPH A

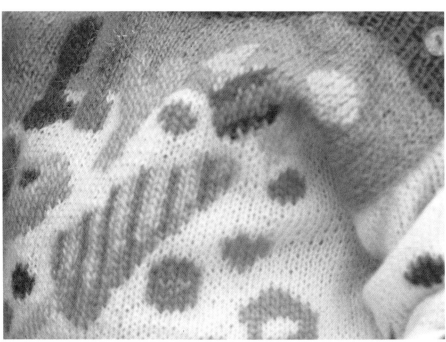	

- ● C1 red
- ○ C2 blue
- = C3 apricot
- · C4 beige
- ✕ C5 hot pink
- − C6 pink
- ∨ C7 yellow
- ⁒ C8 grey

GRAPH B

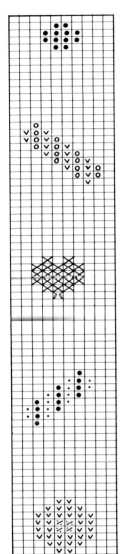

●	C1 red
⊙	C2 blue
⊟	C3 apricot
·	C4 beige
⊠	C5 hot pink
−	C6 pink
∨	C7 yellow
⊡	C8 grey

'KITTY AND TOM'
Jumper

To fit ages 6yrs, 8yrs, 10yrs

Materials

Mohair	50g balls 8 ply
Main Colour (MC) (white)	2 (2,2) balls
1st Contrast (C1) (pale blue)	2 (2,2) balls
2nd Contrast (C2) (dark blue)	2 (2,2) balls

1 ball each of C3 (grey);
C4 (pale grey), C5
(green); C6 (black); C7
(tan) and C8 (pink)
One pair each 3.75mm and 3mm
needles; stitch holder.

Measurements

Garment measures	70	74	79	cm
Back length	40	45	50	cm
Sleeve seam	29	32	35	cm

TENSION
22 sts and 30 rows to 10 cm over
st st on 3.75mm needles.
**IT IS IMPORTANT TO KNIT A
TENSION SQUARE AND TO
WORK TO STATED TENSION IN
ORDER TO OBTAIN REQUIRED
MEASUREMENTS. IF YOUR
SQUARE IS BIGGER USE FINER
NEEDLES. IF YOUR SQUARE IS
SMALLER USE THICKER
NEEDLES.**

Back

Using 3mm needles and MC, cast on 66
(70,74) sts.
Rib k1, p1 for 4.5 (4.5,5) cm, inc 13
(13,15) sts evenly along last row to 79
(83,89) sts. *
Change to 3.75mm needles and st st until
work meas 40 (45,50) cm from beg,
ending with wsr.

Shape shoulders

Cast off 12 (12,13) sts at beg of next 2
rows then cast off 12 (13,14) sts at beg of
next 2 rows. Slip rem 31 (33,35) sts onto
holder.

Front

Cast on and work as for Back to *
Change to 3.75mm needles, st st and beg
chart where indicated for your size. Work
chart from right to left on k rows and left
to right on p rows.
Carry yarn across back of work, taking
care to keep tension even — if taking
yarn across more than 8 sts, use
separate ball of yarn, twisting each yarn
used with next to avoid holes. When chart
has been completed cont until work meas
35 (39,44.5) cm from beg, ending with
wsr.

Shape neck

Keeping chart correct, patt 31 (32,34) sts,
turn. On these sts only, cast off 3 sts at
beg of next row.
Work 1 row.
Cast off 2 sts at beg of next row then 1
st at beg of foll 2 alt rows. 24 (25,27) sts.
Cont to work from chart until front
matches back to shoulder, ending with
wsr.

Shape shoulder

Cast off 12 (12,13) sts at beg of next row.
Work 1 row.
Cast off rem 12 (13,14) sts.
Return to rem sts. Slip centre 17 (19,21)
sts onto holder, rejoin yarn at neck edge.
Cont to work from chart, work 2nd half to
match, shaping in reverse.

Sleeves

Using 3mm needles and MC, cast on 40
(42,44) sts.
Rib as for Back for 3 (3.5,4) cm, inc 9
(10,11) sts evenly along last row to 49
(52,55) sts. Break off MC.
Using 3.75mm needles, C2 and st st, inc
1 st each end of 3rd and every foll 4th
row to 75 (80,85) sts, AT SAME TIME
work 38 rows in C2 and break off yarn.
Join in C1, cont to inc as before, work 30
rows and break off yarn.
Join in MC and cont until work meas 29
(32,35) cm from beg, ending with wsr.
Cast off loosely.

To Make Up

Using backstitch to sew all seams. Sew
buttons on Back to correspond with
buttonholes on Front of garment. Fit
sleeve tops and sew with a stretch stitch.
Join side and sleeve seams. Do not
press.

Even the most expert knitter will
occasionally knit a purl stitch or
purl a knit one. It is quite easy to
correct errors like this without
resorting to unravelling the whole
section. The simplest way is to
drop the stitch immediately above
the one to be changed and allow it
to ladder down to it. Then with your
crochet hook it is quite a simple
matter to work back up to the
needle again.

Neckband

Join right shoulder seam. With rsf, using 3mm needles and C2, pick up and k94 (98,102) sts evenly around neck edge (including sts from stitch holders). Beg with a 2nd row, work in rib as for Back until rib meas 8 cm from beg.
Cast off loosely in rib.

To Make Up

Join left shoulder and neckband seam. Fold neckband in half, to inside and slipstitch into position. Place markers 16.5 (18,19) cm down each side of shoulder seam for armholes. Fit sleeve tops between markers, sew with a stretchy stitch. Do not cramp sleeve tops, spread further if necessary. Join side and sleeve seams. Using a darning needle and black yarn embroider cat's whiskers and lashes as illustrated. Do not press.

NOTE: When changing colours in centre of row, twist the colour to be used underneath and to the right of colour just used, making sure both yarns are worked firmly at joins. Always change colours on wrong side of work so colour changes do not show on right side. Use a separate ball of yarn for each section of colour. We suggest using bobbins. Wind a quantity of yarn around bobbin and place end through slot to hold. Unwind only enough yarn to knit required sts, then place yarn in slot, keeping bobbin close to work.

☐	MC white
—	C1 light blue
⊠	C2 blue
·	C3 grey
⁄	C4 pale grey
⋁	C5 green
■	C6 black
=	C7 tan
⊙	C8 pink

8yrs,

10yrs, 6yrs,

Centre st

8yrs,

6yrs, 10yrs,

ZOO FRIENDS
Jumper

To fit ages 4yrs, 6yrs, 8yrs

Materials

50g balls 8 ply
Main Colour (MC)
(turquoise)   6 (7,7) balls
1st Contrast (C1) (white) 2 (2,2) balls
1 ball each of C2 (red);
C3 (yellow); C4 (pink);
C5 (blue); C6 (black); C7
(brown); C8 (beige); C9
(grey)
One pair each 4mm and 3.25mm
needles; stitch holders.

Measurements

Garment measures	71	75	79 cm
Back length	38	42.5	46 cm
Sleeve seam	27.5	30.5	33.5 cm

TENSION
21 sts and 26 rows to 10 cm over
st st on 4mm needles.
**IT IS IMPORTANT TO KNIT A
TENSION SQUARE AND TO
WORK TO STATED TENSION IN
ORDER TO OBTAIN REQUIRED
MEASUREMENTS. IF YOUR
SQUARE IS BIGGER USE FINER
NEEDLES. IF YOUR SQUARE IS
SMALLER USE THICKER
NEEDLES.**

Back

Using 3.25mm needles and C2, cast on
64 (66,68) sts.
Rib k1, p1 for 4 (4.5,5) cm, inc 14 (15,17)
sts evenly along last row to 78 (81,85)
sts. Break off C2. **
Using 4mm needles and MC st st
throughout, work 10 rows.
Break off MC. Using C1, work 13 rows.
Break off C1.
Join MC and cont straight until work
meas 38 (42.5,46) cm from beg, ending
with wsr.

Shape shoulders
Cast off 11 (12,12) sts at beg of next 2
rows. Cast off 12 (12,13) sts at beg of
next 2 rows. Slip rem 32 (33,35) sts onto
holder.

Front

Cast on and work as for Back to **
Change to 4mm needles, join MC and
work 6 rows.
Set chart on next row as follows. Work
chart from right to left on k rows, and left
to right on p rows. Do not weave
contrasts but carry across back of work
taking care to keep tension even. Use a
separate ball for each C, twisting last C
used with next to link sts.
1st row: k46 (47,49) MC, k1 C4, k MC to
end.
2nd row: p30 (32,34) MC, p2 C4, p MC
to end.
Complete chart as set from 3rd row and

cont until work meas 33 (37.5,41) cm
from beg, ending with wsr.

Shape neck
k28 (29,30) sts, turn. On these sts only,
cast off 2 sts at neck edge on next row.
Work 1 row. Dec 1 st at neck edge on
next and foll 2 alt rows. 23 (24,25) sts.
Cont from chart until Front matches Back
to shoulder, ending at armhole edge.

Shape shoulder
Cast off 11 (12,12) sts at beg of next row.
Work 1 row. Cast off rem 12 (12,13) sts.
Return to rem sts, slip centre 22 (23,25)
sts on holder. Rejoin yarn at neck edge,
work 2nd half to match, shaping in
reverse.

Sleeves

Using 3.25mm needles and C3, cast on 44 (46,48) sts.
Rib k1, p1 for 3 (3.5,4) cm, inc 13 sts evenly along last row to 57 (59,61) sts. Break off C3.
Change to 4mm needles and MC work in st st, inc 1 st each end of 3rd and every foll 4th row to 75 (79,83) sts, AT SAME TIME, when work meas 19 (21.5,24) cm from beg, ending with wsr, join C1 and work 4 rows. Break off C1, join C6 and work 2 rows. Break off C6.
Using MC, cont straight until work meas 27.5 (30.5,33.5) cm from beg, ending with wsr. Cast off loosely.

Neckband

Join right shoulder seam. With rsf, using 3.25mm needles and C4, pick up and k82 (86,90) sts evenly around neck edge, including sts from holders. Beg with a 2nd row, work in rib until rib meas 12 cm from beg. Cast off loosely in rib.

To Make Up

Join left shoulder and neckband seam. Fold neckband in half to inside and slipstitch into place. Place markers 16.5 (17.5,18.5) cm down each side of shoulder seams for armholes. Fit sleeve tops between markers. Sew with a stretchy st. Do not cramp sleeve tops, spread further if necessary. Join side and sleeve seams. Press lightly on wrong side of garment using warm iron and damp cloth.

Symbol	Colour	Symbol	Colour
⊡	C1 white	O	C7 brown
●	C2 red	I	C8 beige
╱	C3 yellow	=	C9 grey
∴	C4 pink	5 — M	
⊠	C5 blue	6 — white	
■	C6 black		

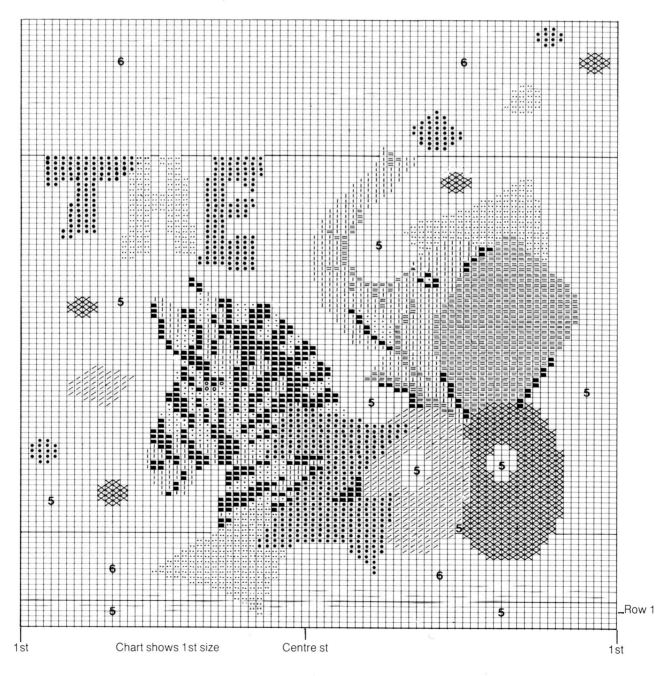

1st   Chart shows 1st size   Centre st   1st

Row 1

CHOPPER PILOT
Jumper

To fit ages 4yrs, 6yrs, 8yrs

Materials

50g balls 8 ply

Main Colour (MC) (sky
blue)   4 (5,5) balls
1st Contrast (C1) (dark
blue)   4 (4,4) balls
1 ball each of C2
(mustard); C3 (cherry
red); C4 (orange red);
C5 (black); C6 (yellow)
and C7 (light grey).
8th Contrast (C8)
(turquoise)   4 (4,4) balls
9th Contrast (C9) (white) 1 (1,1) ball
One pair each 4mm and 3.25mm
needles; 2 stitch holders.

Measurements

Garment measures	68	72	77	cm
Back length	39	41	47	cm
Sleeve seam	29	30.5	32	cm

TENSION

21 sts and 26 rows to 10 cm over
st st on 4mm needles.
**IT IS IMPORTANT TO KNIT A
TENSION SQUARE AND TO
WORK TO STATED TENSION IN
ORDER TO OBTAIN REQUIRED
MEASUREMENTS. IF YOUR
SQUARE IS BIGGER USE FINER
NEEDLES. IF YOUR SQUARE IS
SMALLER USE THICKER
NEEDLES.**

Back

Using 3.25mm needles and C3, cast on
60 (64,68) sts.

Rib k1, p1 for 4 (4,5) cm, inc 12 sts
evenly along last row to 72 (76,80) sts.
Break off C3.
Change to 4mm needles. **
Using C1 and C8 beg and end Chart A
where indicated for your size, working in
st st throughout. Work chart from right to
left on k rows and left to right on p rows.
Rep chart until work meas 39 (41,43) cm
from beg, ending with wsr.

◥ MC		◥ C5	
= C1		I C6	
◿ C2		☐ C7	
⌐ C3		◿ C8	
◤ C4		▾ C9	

1 — M   2 — C1   3 — C7   4 — C8

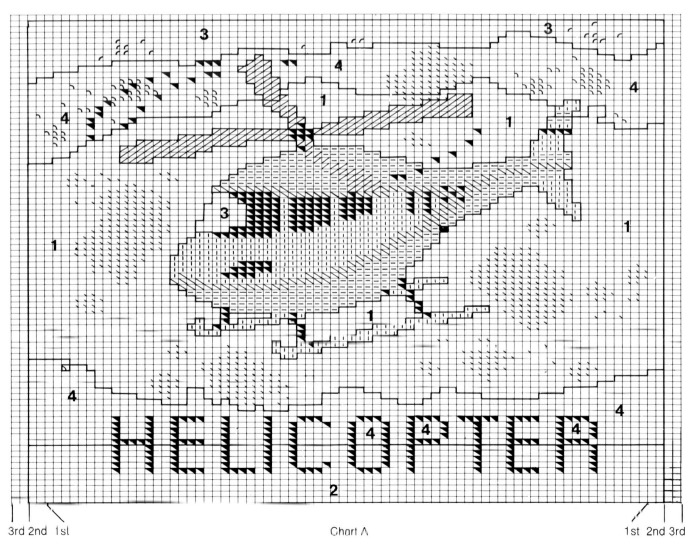

3rd 2nd 1st   Chart A   1st 2nd 3rd

Shape shoulders

Keeping patt correct, cast off 11 sts at beg of next 2 rows.
Cast off 11 (12,13) sts at beg of next 2 rows. Slip rem 28 (30,32) sts onto holder.

Front

Cast on and work as for Back to **
Using C1, work 2 (4,6) rows st st, then commence Chart B, using separate balls of C, twisting last C used with next to link sts and taking care to keep tension even. Beg and end where indicated for your size. Complete chart and cont in C7 until work meas 34 (36,38) cm from beg, ending with wsr.

Shape neck

k27 (28,29) sts, turn. On these sts only, cast off 2 sts at neck edge.
Dec 1 st at neck edge on next and foll 2 alt rows. 22 (23,24) sts.
Cont straight until Front matches Back to shoulder, ending at armhole edge.

Shape shoulder

Cast off 11 sts at beg of next row. Work 1 row.
Cast off rem 11 (12,13) sts. Return to rem sts, slip centre 18 (20,22) sts on holder. Rejoin yarn at neck edge, work 2nd half to match, shaping in reverse.

Chart B

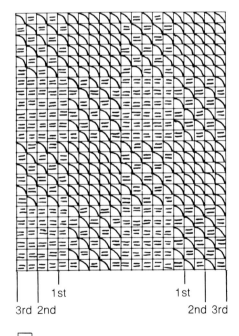

1st   1st

3rd 2nd   2nd 3rd

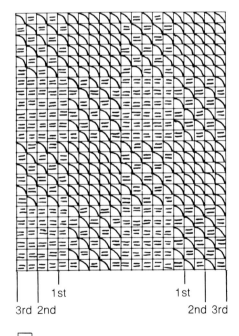 MC

C1

Sleeves

Using 3.25mm needles and C6, cast on 40 (42,44) sts.
Rib k1, p1 for 5 cm, inc 14 sts evenly along last row to 54 (56,58) sts.
Break off C6.
Change to 4mm needles.
Using C1 and C8, working from Chart B, beg and ending patt as indicated.
Inc 1 st at each end of 3rd and every foll 4th row to 72 (74,78) sts, working extra sts into patt. Cont straight until work meas 29 (30.5,32) cm from beg, ending with wsr.
Cast off loosely.

Neckband

Join right shoulder seam. With rsf, using 3.25mm needles and C2, pick up and k72 (74,76) sts evenly around neck edge, including sts from holders. Work in rib until rib meas 10 cm from beg. Cast off loosely in rib.

To Make Up

Join left shoulder and neckband seam. Place markers 17.5 (18,18.5) cm each side of shoulder seam for armholes. Fit sleeve tops between markers, sew with a stretchy st. Do not cramp sleeve tops, spread further if necessary. Join side and sleeve seams. Fold neckband in half to inside and slipstitch into place. Press garment lightly on wrong side, with warm iron and damp cloth.

Some knitted pieces will require pressing on the wrong side with a damp cloth and an iron temperature suitable for the yarn fibre. Never slide the iron to and fro across the knitting as this tends to distort the shape. It is enough to place the iron on the knitting and then lift it straight up before placing it down on another area.

FIREFIGHTER
Jumper

To fit ages 4yrs, 6yrs, 8yrs

Materials

50g balls 5 ply
Main Colour (MC) —
blue   2 (2,2) balls
1 ball each of C1 (light
grey); C2 (dark green);
C3 (light green); C4 (mid
blue); C5 (pale blue); C6
(black); C7 (white); C8
(yellow); C9 (tan); C10
(cherry red).
2 balls C11 (orange
red).
1 ball each C12 (grey)
and C13 (beige).
One pair each 3.75mm and 3mm
needles; stitch holder.

Measurements

Garment measures	68	73	78	cm
Back length	36	41	45	cm
Sleeve seam	26	29	32	cm

TENSION
26 sts to 10 cm over st st.
**IT IS IMPORTANT TO KNIT A
TENSION SQUARE AND TO
WORK TO STATED TENSION IN
ORDER TO OBTAIN REQUIRED
MEASUREMENTS. IF YOUR
SQUARE IS BIGGER USE FINER
NEEDLES. IF YOUR SQUARE IS
SMALLER USE THICKER
NEEDLES.**

Back

Using 3mm needles and MC, cast on 80
(82,84) sts.
Rib k1, p1 for 4 (5,6) cm, inc 10 (14,18)
sts evenly along last row to 90 (96,102)
sts. Break off MC. **
Change to 3.75mm needles and patt as
follows:
1st row: using C10, p to end.
2nd row: k.
3rd row: k8 (0,2) C10, p2 (1,2) C11, *
k10 C10, p2 C11, rep from * ending last
rep with k8 (10,2) C10, p0 (1,0) C11.
4th row: k0 (1,0) C11, p8 (10,2) C10, * k2
C11, p10 C10, rep from * ending last rep

with k2 (1,2) C11, p8 (0,2) C10.
Rep 3rd and 4th rows 4 times.
13th row: as 1st row.
14th row: as 2nd row.
15th row: k2 (5,8) C10, * p2 C11, k10
C10, rep from * ending last rep with p2
C11, k2 (5,8) C10.
16th row: p2 (5,8) C10, * k2 C11, p10
C10, rep from * ending last rep with k2
C11, p2 (5,8) C10.
Rep 15th and 16th rows 4 times.
These 24 rows form patt. Rep patt as
necessary until work meas 36 (41,45) cm
from beg, ending with wsr.

Shape shoulders
Keeping patt correct, cast off 13 (14,15)
sts at beg of next 4 rows. Place rem 38
(40,42) sts onto holder.

Sleeves

Using 3mm needles and MC, cast on 44
(46,48) sts.
Rib k1, p1 for 4 (4,5) cm, inc 20 sts
evenly along last row of rib.
64 (66,68) sts.
Break off MC.
Change to 3.75mm needles and set patt
as follows:
1st row: using C10, p to end.

2nd row: p to end.
3rd row: k7 (8,9) C10, * p2 C11, k10
C10, rep from * ending last rep with p2
C11, k7 (8,9) C10.
4th row: p7 (8,9) C10, * k2 C11, p10
C10, rep from * ending last rep with k2
C11, p7 (8,9) C10.
Cont in patt as set, inc 1 st each end of
3rd and every foll 4th row to
80 (90,96) sts, working extra sts into patt.
Cont straight until work meas 26
(29,32) cm from beg, or required length,
ending with wsr. Cast off loosely.

⊟	orange red
⊠	cherry red

Sleeves / Back

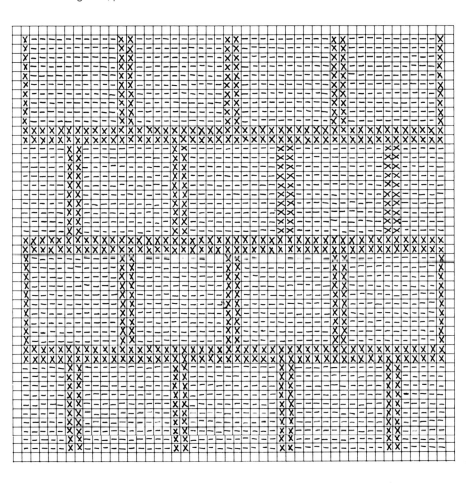

3rd 2nd 1st
size

1st 2nd 3rd
size

Front

Cast on and work as for Back to **
Change to 3.75mm needles and begin
chart. Work chart from right to left on k
rows, and from left to right on p rows.
When working chart use separate balls of
Contrasts, twisting last C used with next
to link sts, taking care to keep tension
even. Complete chart and work 6 (12,18)
rows in C5. Break off C5 and cont in MC
until work meas 31 (36,39) cm from beg,
ending with wsr.

Shape neck

k38 (41,44) sts, turn. On these sts only,
cast off 4 sts once, 3 sts once, 2 sts
twice, and dec 1 st 1 (2,3) times at neck
edge on next and foll alt rows. 26 (28,30)
sts.
Cont straight until front matches back to
shoulder, ending at armhole edge.

Shape shoulder

Cast off 13 (14,15) sts beg of next and foll
alt row. Fasten off.

Return to rem sts, slip centre 14 sts onto
holder. Rejoin yarn at neck edge, work
2nd half to match, shaping in reverse.

Neckband

Join right shoulder seam. With rsf, using
3mm needles and MC, pick up and k90
(92,94) sts evenly around neck edge,
including sts from holders. Work in rib
until rib meas 7 cm from beg. Cast off
loosely in rib.

To Make Up

Join left shoulder and neckband seam.
Place markers 16 (17,18) cm each side of
shoulder seam for armholes. Fit sleeves
between markers and sew with a stretchy
stitch. Do not cramp sleeve tops, spread
further if necessary. Join side and sleeve
seams. Fold neckband in half to inside,
slipstitch into place. Press garment
lightly, on wrong side, using warm iron
and damp cloth.

Symbol	Colour		
I	tan	1 — white
⧄	light grey	2 — green
◣	black	3 — light green
−	orange red	4 — light blue
◲	cherry red	5 — mid blue
⊠	blue MC	
◺	skin colour	
⌐	yellow	
⟋	white	
◪	mid blue	
◳	green	
=	light green	
•	dark grey	

Cable Stitch

The look and texture of the cable pattern has long been a favourite with knitters. The method is quite simple. A number of stitches from the left-hand needle are held at the front or back of the work on a cable needle while the same number of stitches are worked from the left-hand needle. The stitches are then worked from the cable needle producing the twisted effect.* It is important when knitting cables to keep an exact row count so that the twists are evenly spaced.

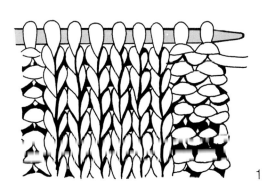

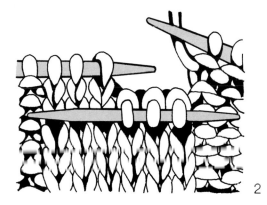

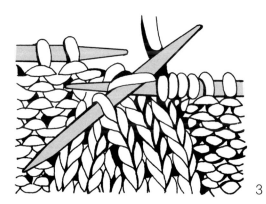

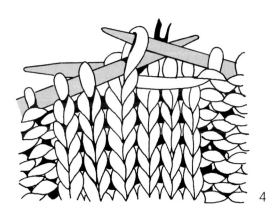

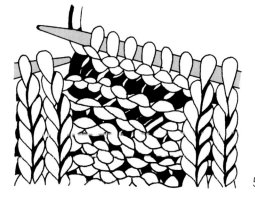

* Using a cable needle a size or two smaller than your knitting needles will make it easier to slide your cable stitches back and forth without stretching them.

Nautical Notes

Sail away on a blue water adventure
with these nautical picture jumpers. The
ever-popular motif of Anchors Away, in 8 ply with
convenient shoulder openings, will brighten up the
smart set. The little ones aren't left out, with
a charming design in 4 ply cotton for
cool summer evenings.

BLUE WATER ADVENTURES
Jumpers

To fit ages 2yrs, 4yrs, 6yrs

Materials

Cleckheaton	50g balls 8 ply

Boat Neck Jumper

Main Colour (MC)	2 (2,3) balls
1st Contrast (C1)	1 (2,2) ball/s
2nd Contrast (C2)	1 (1,1) ball
3rd Contrast (C3)	1 (2,2) ball/s
4th Contrast (C4)	1 (1,1) ball

Round Neck Jumper

Main Colour (MC)	4 (5,5) balls
1st Contrast (C1)	1 (2,2) ball/s
2nd Contrast (C2)	1 (1,1) ball
3rd Contrast (C3)	1 (1,2) ball/s
4th Contrast (C4)	1 (1,1) ball

One pair each 4mm and 3.25mm, and set of 3.25mm needles, 2 stitch holders for Jumper with Round Neck; bobbins, tapestry needle for embroidery, 4 buttons for Jumper with Boat Neck.

Measurements

Garment measures	61	66	72	cm
Back length	32	37	41	cm
Sleeve seam	21	25	31	cm

JUMPER WITH BOAT NECK

Back

Using 3.25 mm needles and MC cast on 63(69,75) sts.

Where a picture or pattern needs to be worked it is often given in the form of a graph or chart where each square represents one stitch and one row of knitting. Knit rows on the graph are worked from right to left and purl rows from left to right. The various colours to be worked are usually indicated by different symbols and care should be taken to work exactly as the graph indicates, perhaps by ticking off rows as they are completed.

1st row: k2 * p1, k1, rep from * to last st, k1.
2nd row: k1 * p1, k1, rep from * to end.
Work 4 more rows rib (MC). Work 4 rows rib C3. Work 6 rows rib (MC), inc 5 sts evenly across last row. 68(74, 80) sts.
Change to 4mm needles. **
Work 36 rows st st in stripes of 6 rows C1, 6 rows C2, 6 rows C1, 4 rows C2, 4 rows MC and 10 rows C1.***
Using MC, cont in st st until work meas 30 (35,39)cm from beg, ending with a purl row and dec one st in centre of last row. 67 (73,79) sts.
Using C1, **next row:** knit.
Work 5 rows rib in C1 as for lower band (beg with a 2nd row).

Divide for back shoulder bands
Next row: rib 22 (24,26), cast off next 23 (25,27) sts, rib 22 (24,26).
Cont on last 22 (24,26) sts until shoulder band meas 2cm from beg, ending with a 2nd row.
Cast off loosely in rib.
Join yarn to rem sts and complete other side to correspond.

Front

Work as for back to **.
Work rows 1 to 61 inclusive from Graph.
****
Using MC, cont in st st (beg with a purl row) until work meas 30 (35,39)cm from beg, ending with a purl row, and dec one st in centre of last row. 67 (73,79) sts.
Using C1, **next row:** knit.
Work 1 row rib as for lower band, beg with a 2nd row.
Next row: rib 2 (3,4), cast off 2 sts, rib 14, cast off 2 sts, rib 27 (31,35), cast off 2 sts, rib 14, cast off 2 sts, rib 2 (3,4).
Next row: rib 2 (3,4), cast on 2 sts, rib 14, cast on 2 sts, rib 27 (31,35), cast on 2 sts, rib 14, cast on 2 sts, rib 2 (3,4).
Work 2 rows rib.
Cast off loosely in rib.

Left Sleeve

Using 3.25mm needles and C3, cast on 37 (39,41) sts.
Work in rib as for lower band until band meas 3cm from beg, ending with a 2nd row and inc 5 sts evenly across last row.

42 (44,46) sts.
Change to 4mm needles.
Cont in st st and stripes of 8 rows MC and 8 rows C3 throughout, inc one st at each end of 5th and foll 4th (6th,4th) row / s until there are 50 (62,50) sts. 1st and 3rd sizes only — inc 1st at each end of 6th rows until there are 58 (62,70) sts.
Cont in stripes without shaping until side edge meas 31 (36,41)cm from beg, ending with a purl row.

Shape sleeve top
Cast off 8 (8,10) sts at beg of next 4 rows, then 7 (9,9) sts at beg of foll 2 rows.
Cast off rem sts.

Right Sleeve

Work as for left sleeve using C1 in place of C3.

•	C3
⊠	C4
◿	MC

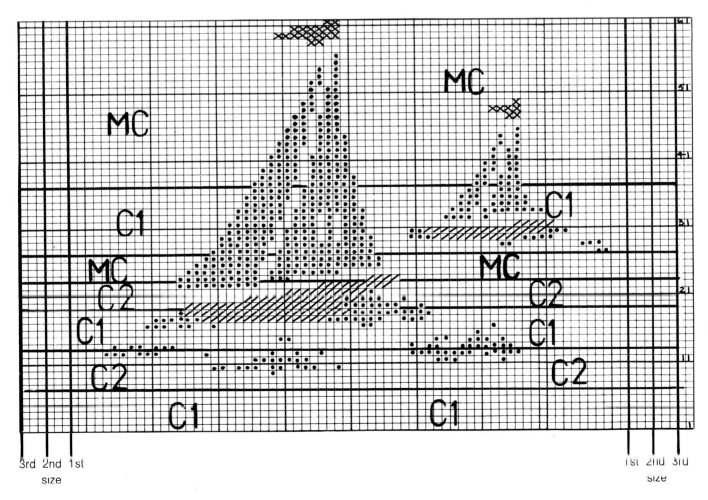

To Make Up

Overlap front shoulder band over back shoulder band, matching shoulder seams and slip stitch in position at sleeve edge. Sew in sleeves placing centre of sleeves to shoulder seams. Join side and sleeve seams. Sew on buttons. Using C3 and knitting stitch, embroider waves on back as shown on Graph, across stripes.

TENSION

22 sts to 10cm over st st, using 4mm needles.

IT IS IMPORTANT TO KNIT A TENSION SQUARE AND TO WORK TO STATED TENSION IN ORDER TO OBTAIN REQUIRED MEASUREMENTS. IF YOUR SQUARE IS BIGGER USE FINER NEEDLES. IF YOUR SQUARE IS SMALLER USE THICKER NEEDLES.

JUMPER WITH ROUND NECK

Back

Work as for back of Boat Neck Jumper to ***
Using MC cont in st st until work meas 32 (37,41)cm from beg, ending with a purl row.

Shape shoulders
Cast off 7 (8,9) sts at beg of next 4 rows, then 8 sts at beg of foll 2 rows.
Leave rem 24 (26, 28) sts on a stitch holder.

Front

Work as for front of Boat Neck Jumper to ****
Using MC, cont in st st until there are 18 (20,22) rows less than back to shoulder shaping.

Shape neck
Next row: k26 (29,32), turn.
Dec one st at neck edge in foll alt rows until 22 (24,26) sts rem.
Work 9 rows.

Shape shoulder
Cast off 7 (8,9) sts at beg of next and foll alt row.
Work 1 row.
Cast off.
Slip next 16 sts onto a stitch holder and

leave. Join yarn to rem sts and complete to correspond with other side.

Left and Right Sleeve

Work as for left and right sleeve of Boat Neck Jumper.

Neckband

Using back stitch, join shoulder seams. With rsf, using set of 3.25mm needles and MC, beg at left shoulder seam, knit up 78 (84,90) sts evenly around neck edge (including sts from stitch holders). Using C1, **1st round:** *k1, p1, rep from * to end.
Rep 1st round until band meas 4cm from beg.
Cast off loosely in rib.

To Make Up

Sew in sleeves placing centre of sleeves to shoulder seams. Sew side and sleeve seams. Using C3 and knitting stitch, embroider waves on back as shown on Graph across stripes. Fold neckband in half onto wrong side and slip stitch in position.

NOTE: When changing colours in centre of row, twist the colour to be used underneath and to the right of colour just used, making sure both yarns are worked firmly at joins. Use a separate ball of yarn for each section of colour. We suggest using bobbins.

Before a garment can be completed it is usual for the pieces to be pressed and sometimes blocked. Ribbing is never pressed or blocked in order to retain its elasticity and highly textured patterns rarely are. Stocking stitch is usually pressed and often blocked. Be guided by the pattern instructions and the information on the paper band around the balls of yarn.

SAIL AWAY
Jumper

To fit ages 3yrs, 4yrs, 5yrs

Materials

Cotton   50g balls 4 ply
Main Colour (MC)   3 balls
1 ball each of 4 contrast
colours (C1, C2, C3 and
C4)
One pair each 3.25mm and 2.75mm
needles; stitch holder.

Measurements

Garment measures	60	65	70	cm
Back length	32	37	42	cm
Sleeve seam	24	32	37	cm

Back

Using 2.75mm needles and C1, cast on
80 (88,96) sts.
Rib k1, p1 for 4 cm, inc 5 sts evenly along
last row to 85 (93,101) sts.
Change to 3.25mm needles and st st. **
Patt as follows:
* Work 2 rows C1 and 2 rows MC. Rep
from * 9 (10,11) times.
Break off C1 and cont in MC until work
meas 19 (23,27) cm from beg, ending
with wsr.

Shape armholes

Cast off 6 (7,8) sts beg of next 2 rows.
Cont straight until Back meas 30
(35,40) cm from beg, ending with wsr.

TENSION
28 sts and 37 rows to 10 cm over
st st on 3.25mm needles.
**IT IS IMPORTANT TO KNIT A
TENSION SQUARE AND TO
WORK TO STATED TENSION IN
ORDER TO OBTAIN REQUIRED
MEASUREMENTS. IF YOUR
SQUARE IS BIGGER USE FINER
NEEDLES. IF YOUR SQUARE IS
SMALLER USE THICKER
NEEDLES.**

☐ M

☒ C1

☒ C2

⊡ C3

◉ C4

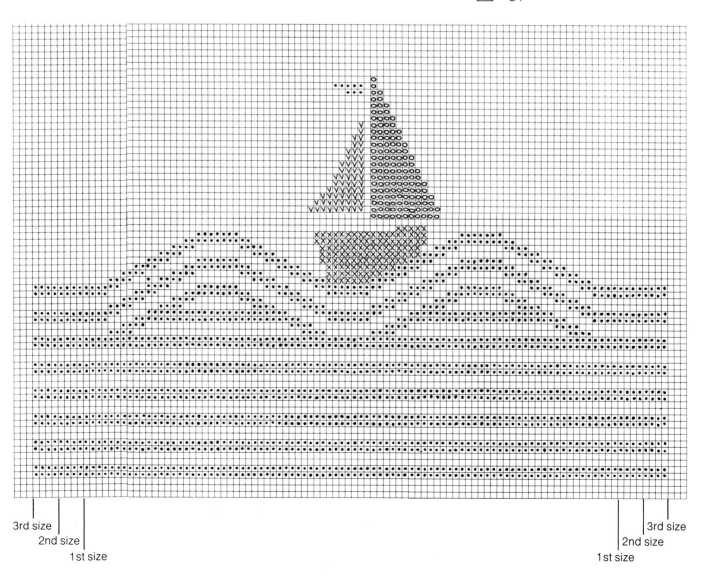

3rd size
2nd size
1st size

3rd size
2nd size
1st size

Shape neck

k25 (26,27) sts, turn. On these sts only, cast off 3 sts once and 2 sts once at neck edge on next and foll alt row.
Cont straight until work meas 32 (37,43) cm from beg, ending at armhole edge. Cast off loosely.
Return to rem sts, slip centre 23 (27,31) sts onto holder. Rejoin yarn at neck edge, work 2nd half to match, shaping in reverse.

Front

Cast on and work as for Back to **
Working in stripe patt as for Back, rep from * 6 (7,8) times.
Begin working from chart where indicated for your size.
Work chart from right to left on k rows and left to right on p rows. Carry MC across back of work, taking care to keep tension even — if taking yarn across more than 8 sts, use separate balls of MC, twisting yarns to link sts when changing colour to avoid holes.
When work meas 19 (23,27) cm from beg, ending with wsr.

Shape armholes

Work as for Back, keeping chart correct. When chart has been completed, break off contrast yarns and cont in MC, until work meas 27 (31,36) cm from beg, ending with wsr.

Shape neck

k30 (31,32) sts, turn. On these sts only, cast off at neck edge 3 sts once, 2 sts twice and 1 st 3 times on next and foll alt rows. Cont straight until Front matches Back to shoulder, ending at armhole edge.
Cast off loosely.
Return to rem sts, slip centre 13 (17,21) sts onto holder.
Rejoin yarn at neck edge and work 2nd half to match, shaping in reverse.

Sleeves

Using 2.75mm needles and MC, cast on 36 (38,40) sts.
Rib k1, p1 for 4 cm, inc 10 (14,18) sts evenly along last row to 46 (52,58) sts.
Change to 3.25mm needles and st st. Inc 1 st each end of 3rd and every foll 4th row to 68 (74,80) sts. Cont straight until work meas 24 (32,37) cm from beg, ending with wsr. Cast off loosely.

Neckband

Join right shoulder seam. With rsf, using 2.75mm needles and MC, pick up and k84 (90,96) sts evenly around neck, including sts from holders. Work in rib until rib meas 4 cm from beg. Cast off loosely in rib.

To Make Up

Join left shoulder and neckband seam. Sew in sleeves. Join side and sleeve seams. Do not press.

ANCHORS AWAY
Jumper

To fit ages 4yrs, 6yrs, 8yrs

Materials

Cleckheaton 8 ply Machine Wash 50g balls
Main Colour (MC)   4 (5,6) balls
Contrast (C)   1 ball
One pair each 4mm and 3.25mm
needles, 3 stitch holders, 4 buttons

Measurements

Garment measurement	60	76	82	cm
Back length approx	38	42	46	cm
Sleeve seam (approx)	27	32	36	cm

TENSION
22 sts to 10 cm over st st on 4mm needles.

IT IS IMPORTANT TO KNIT A TENSION SQUARE AND TO WORK TO STATED TENSION IN ORDER TO OBTAIN REQUIRED MEASUREMENTS. IF YOUR SQUARE IS BIGGER USE FINER NEEDLES. IF YOUR SQUARE IS SMALLER USE THICKER NEEDLES.

Back

Using 3.25mm needles and C, cast on 71 (79,87) sts.
Using MC, **1st row:** k2, *p1, k1, rep from * to last st, k1.
2nd row: k1, *p1, k1, rep from * to end.
Rep 1st and 2nd rows until work meas 3 (4,4) cm from beg, ending with a 2nd row and inc 6 sts evenly across last row. 77 (85,93) sts.
Change to 4mm needles.
Using MC, work 0 (0,8) rows st st.**
Using C, work 0 (2,2) rows st st.
Using MC, work 8 (14,14) rows st. st.
Work 80 rows st st in stripes of 2 rows C, and 14 rows MC.
Using C, work 2 rows st st.
Using MC, work 10 (12,16) rows st st, inc 12 sts evenly across last row. 89 (97,105) sts.
Change to 3.25mm needles and C.
Knit one row.

Next row: k1, *p1, k1, rep from * to end.
Using MC, work 8 rows rib as for lower band.
Cast off loosely in rib.

Front

Work as for Back to **.
Work rows 9 (1,1) to 102 (104,108) inclusive from Graph.

Shape neck
Using MC, **next row:** k29 (33,36), turn.
Dec one st at neck edge in every row until 25 (29,32) sts rem.
Work 1 row, inc 4 sts evenly across row. 29 (33,36) sts.
Leave rem sts on a stitch holder.
Slip next 19 (19,21) sts onto a stitch holder and leave. Join yarn to rem sts and complete other side of neck to correspond.

Front Upper Band

With rsf, using 3.25mm needles and C, knit across sts from left Front stitch holder, knit up 7 sts evenly along left side of neck, knit across 19 (19,21) sts from centre Front stitch holder, knit up 7 sts evenly along right side of neck, then knit across sts from right Front stitch holder. 91 (99,107) sts.
Next row: k1, *p1, k1, rep from * to end.
Using MC, work 4 rows rib.
Next row: rib 11 (13,14), * cast off 2 sts, rib 9 (11,13), cast off 2 sts *, rib 43 (43,45), rep from * to * once, rib 11 (13,14).
Next row: rib 11 (13,14), * cast on 2 sts, rib 9 (11,13), cast on 2 sts *, rib 43 (43,45), rep from * to * once, rib 11 (13,14). (4 buttonholes.)
Work 2 rows rib.
Cast off loosely in rib.

Sleeves

Using 3.25mm needles and C, cast on 35 (35,37) sts.
Using MC, cont in rib as for lower band of Back, until work meas 3 (4,4) cm from beg, ending with a 2nd row and inc 4 (6,6) sts evenly across last row. 39 (41,43) sts.
Change to 4mm needles.
Cont in st st and stripes of 2 rows C, and 14 rows MC throughout, AT SAME TIME inc one st at each end of 5th and foll 4th rows until there are 47 (57,71) sts, then in foll 6th rows until there are 61 (71,79) sts.
Work 11 (11,13) rows.
Cast off loosely.

Cord

Using 4mm needles and MC, cast on 112 sts.
Work 2 rows st st.
Cast off loosely.

To Make Up

Lie Back and Front flat on table so that right sides are facing upwards and front upperbands overlap back upperband. Slip stitch side edges of upperbands together (noting that centre of band is shoulderline). Tie coloured threads 14.5 (16.5, 18.5) cm down from each shoulder. Using backstitch, sew in sleeves evenly between coloured threads, placing centre of sleeves to shoulders. Join side and sleeve seams. Sew on buttons. Thread cord loosely around anchor on Front where indicated on Graph, and as illustrated.

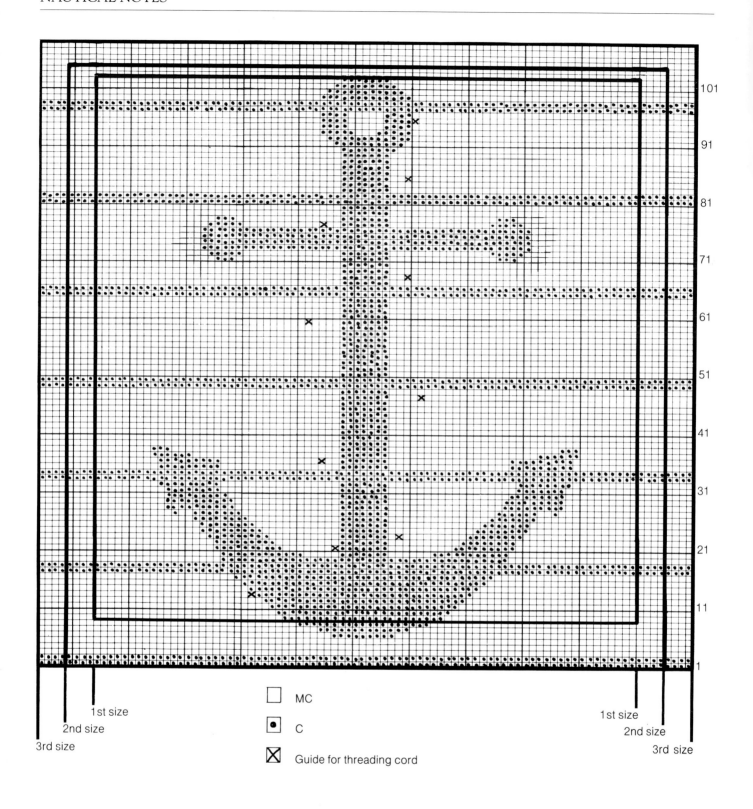

□ MC

⊡ C

☒ Guide for threading cord

1st size

2nd size

3rd size

1st size

2nd size

3rd size

Sporting Days

Whether their game is baseball, cricket
or tennis, these sporting classics will suit any child.
There's a dainty crossover for the young ballerina in
the family and a cardigan with number motif to
suit them on or off the sportsfield.

BASES LOADED
Cardigan

To fit ages 4yrs, 5yrs, 6yrs

Materials

Panda Magnum 8 ply 100 g balls
Main Colour (MC)   2 (2,3) balls
1st Contrast (C1)   1 (1,1) ball
2nd Contrast (C2)   1 (1,1) ball
One pair each 3.25mm and 4mm
needles, 4 buttons.

Measurements

Garment measures	69	75	81	cm
Back length	33	37	41	cm
Sleeve seam	26	31	36	cm

TENSION

22 sts and 30 rows to 10 cm over st st using 4mm needles.
IT IS IMPORTANT TO KNIT A TENSION SQUARE AND TO WORK TO STATED TENSION IN ORDER TO OBTAIN REQUIRED MEASUREMENTS. IF YOUR SQUARE IS BIGGER USE FINER NEEDLES. IF YOUR SQUARE IS SMALLER USE THICKER NEEDLES.

Back

Using 3.25mm needles and C1, cast on 79 (85,93) sts.
1st row: k1, * p1, k1, rep from * to end.
2nd row: p1, * k1, p1, rep from * to end.
Rep 1st and 2nd rows 4 times in stripes of 2 rows each (C2 and C1) twice.

Change to 4mm needles.
Using MC, work 14 (20,26) rows st st.
Work rows 1 to 73 inclusive from Graph, noting to read rs rows from right side of Graph to left and ws rows from left to right.
Using MC, work 3 (9,15) more rows st st beg with a p row.

Shape shoulders

Cast off 9 (10,11) sts at beg of next 4 rows, then 10 (11,12) sts at beg of foll 2 rows.
Cast off rem sts.

NOTE: When changing colour in centre of row, twist the colour to be used underneath and to the right of colour just used. Use a separate ball of yarn for each section of colour. Divide colours into smaller balls as required.

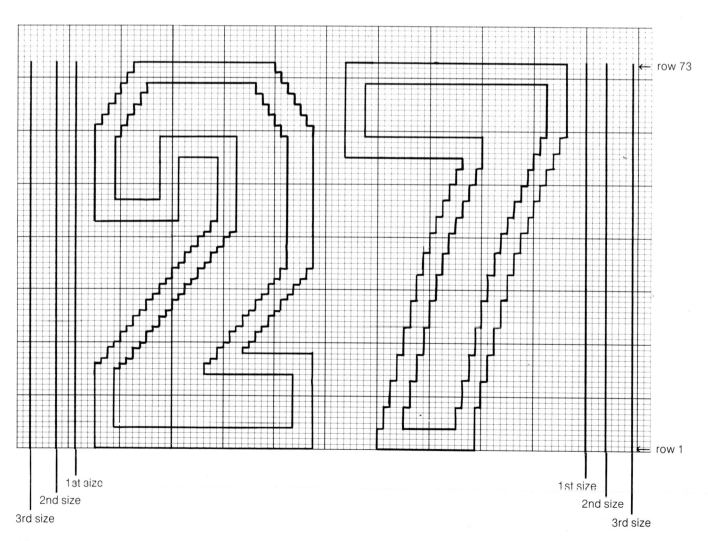

← row 73

← row 1

1st size

2nd size

3rd size

1st size

2nd size

3rd size

Left Front

Using 3.25mm needles and C1, cast on
39 (41,45) sts. Work 10 rows rib in stripes
as for Back, inc one st in centre of last
row. 40 (42,46) sts.
Change to 4mm needles and MC.
Work 40 (48,56) rows st st.

Shape front slope
Dec at end of next and foll 4th rows until
28 (35,39) sts rem. **2nd and 3rd sizes
only:** then in foll 6th rows until (31,34) sts
rem. Work 5 (5,3) rows.

Shape shoulder
Cast off 9 (10,11) sts at beg of next row
and foll alt row. Work 1 row.
Cast off.

Right Front

Work to correspond with Left Front,
reversing shaping.

Right Pocket

Using 4mm needles and MC, cast on 20
sts. Work 19 rows st st.
Cast off 13 sts at beg of next row. Dec at
end of next and at same edge in every row
until 2 sts remain.
Next row: p2tog. Fasten off.
With rsf, using 3.25mm needles and C1,
pick up 27 sts evenly along pocket top.
Work 9 rows rib in stripes as for lower
band.
Cast off.

Left Pocket

Work to correspond with Right Pocket.

Front Band

Join shoulder seams. With rsf, using
3.25mm needles and C1, pick up 90
(102,114) sts evenly across right front,
23 (23,25) sts evenly across back neck,
90 (102,114) sts evenly across left front,
203 (227,253) sts.
Work 3 rows rib in stripes of 1 row C1 and
2 rows C2.
5th row: Using C1 rib to last 41 (47,53)
sts, cast off 2 sts, (rib 10 [12,14], cast off
2 sts) 3 times, rib 3.
6th row: Rib 3, cast on 2 sts (rib10
[12,14], cast on 2 sts) 3 times, rib to end.
Work 4 rows rib in stripes of 2 rows C2
and 2 rows C1.
Cast off.

Sleeves

Tie a marker 48 (54,60) rows down from
shoulders on side edges of fronts and
back. With rsf, using 4mm needles and
MC, pick up 69 (77,87) sts evenly
between markers.
Work in st st, dec at each end of 10th and
foll 6th rows until 53 (59,69) sts rem.
Then in foll 4th rows until 47 (49,51) sts
rem. Work 5 rows.
Change to 3.25mm needles and C1.
Work 10 rows rib in stripes as for lower
band.
Cast off.

To Make Up

Join side and sleeve seams. Stitch
pockets and buttons in position.

Some knitted pieces will require
pressing on the wrong side with a
damp cloth and an iron
temperature suitable for the yarn
fibre. Never slide the iron to and fro
across the knitting as this tends to
distort the shape. It is enough to
place the iron on the knitting and
then lift it straight up before placing
it down on another area.

The same basic technique is
used to work buttonholes, lace
patterns and eyelets. This
involves positioning the yarn
over or around the right hand
needle and following this with a
simple decrease. How the yarn is
positioned generally depends on
where it is to be worked. Between
2 knit stitches or between 2 purl
and a knit stitch, the yarn is
brought to the front of the work
and then over the right hand needle
ready to work the next knit stitch.
This is shown in pattern instructions
as "yfwd". Between 2 purl stitches or
a knit and a purl stitch the yarn is
wrapped around the right hand needle
bringing it to the front again ready to
work the next purl stitch. This is shown in
pattern instructions as "yrn". With
this very simple method you can work
buttonholes, a row of eyelets or a
picot edging for a baby's jacket.

TENNIS ANYONE?
Jumper

To fit ages 6yrs, 8yrs, 10yrs

Materials

Cleckheaton 8 ply Wool Blend Crepe
50g balls

5 (6,7) balls
Small quantity of
yarn for
embroidery

One pair each 3.25mm and 4mm
needles, stitch holder.

Measurements

To fit size	66	71	76	cm
Garment measures	70	77	84	cm
Back length	46	50	54	cm
Sleeve seam	32	35	38	cm

TENSION
22 sts and 26 rows to 10 cm over
st st on 4mm needles.
**IT IS IMPORTANT TO KNIT A
TENSION SQUARE AND TO
WORK TO STATED TENSION IN
ORDER TO OBTAIN REQUIRED
MEASUREMENTS. IF YOUR
SQUARE IS BIGGER USE FINER
NEEDLES. IF YOUR SQUARE IS
SMALLER USE THICKER
NEEDLES.**

Back

Using 3.25mm needles, cast on 60
(68,76) sts.
Rib k1, p1 for 4 cm, inc 17 sts evenly
along last row to 77 (85,93) sts.
Change to 4mm needles and st st until
back meas 46 (50,54) cm from beg,
ending with wsr.
Cast off loosely.

Front

Cast on and work as for Back until work
meas 21 (23,25.5) cm from beg, ending
with wsr.
Dec with a row, work 6 rows reverse st
st

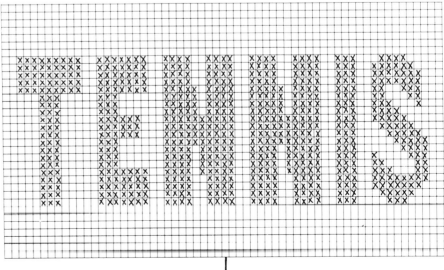

CENTRE STITCH

Set chart on next row as follows:
1st row: p13 (17,21), k3, p4, k3, (p2,k4) 4 times, p2, k7, p5, k3, p to end.
2nd row: k13 (17,21), p3, k5, p7, (k2,p4) 4 times, k2, p3, k4, p3, k to end.
Complete chart as set from 3rd row, then work 6 rows reverse st st. Cont in st st until Front meas 39 (42,46) cm from beg, ending with wsr.

Shape neck

k35 (38,41) sts, turn. On these sts only, cast off 4 sts at beg of next row, 3 sts at beg of foll alt row, 2 sts at beg of foll alt row. Dec 1 st at beg of foll alt rows 3 (5,6) times. 23 (24,26) sts.
Cont straight until Front matches back to shoulder, ending at armhole edge.
Cast off loosely.
Return to rem sts, slip centre 7 (9,11) sts onto holder.
Rejoin yarn at neck edge and work 2nd half to match, shaping in reverse.

Sleeves

Using 3.25mm needles, cast on 34 (36,38) sts.
Rib k1, p1 for 4 cm, inc 12 (12,14) sts evenly along last row. 46 (48,52) sts.
Change to 4mm needles and st st, inc 1 st each end of 3rd and every foll 4th row to 74 (80,86) sts. Cont straight until work meas 32 (35,38) cm from beg, ending with wsr.
Cast off loosely.

Neckband

Join right shoulder seam. With rsf and using 3.25mm needles, pick up and k88 (96,104) sts evenly around neck edge, including sts from holder. Work in rib until rib meas 3 cm from beg.
Cast off loosely in rib.

To Make Up

Join left shoulder and neckband seam. Place markers 19 (20.5,22) cm down each side of shoulder seam for armholes. Fit sleeve tops between markers, sew with a stretchy stitch. Do not cramp sleeve tops, spread further if necessary. Using darning needle and small amount of C yarn, work running st around the word "TENNIS" as illustrated. Do not press.

TWO FOR TENNIS
Jumper

To fit ages 6yrs, 8yrs, 10yrs

Materials

Cleckheaton 8 ply Wool Blend Crepe
50g balls
Main Colour (MC)   6 (6,7) balls
Contrast (C)   1 (1,1) ball
One pair each 4.50mm and 3.25mm
needles; stitch holder.

Measurements

Garment measures	72	80	87	cm
Back length	43	47	51	cm

TENSION
21 sts to 10cm over st st on 4.50mm
needles.
This garment has been designed at
a looser tension than normally
recommended.
**IT IS IMPORTANT TO KNIT A
TENSION SQUARE. IF YOUR
SQUARE IS BIGGER USE FINER
NEEDLES. IF YOUR SQUARE IS
SMALLER USE THICKER
NEEDLES.**

Back

Using 3.25mm needles and MC, cast on
68 (74,80) sts.
Rib k1, p1 for 4 cm, inc 8 (10,12) sts
evenly along last row. 76 (84,92) sts.
Change to 4.50mm needles and st st until
work meas 24 (26,28) cm from beg,
ending with wsr.

Shape armholes
Cast off 0 (0,3) sts at beg of next 0 (0,2)
rows.
Cast off 2 sts at beg of next 4 (4,2) rows.
Dec 1 st each end of next and foll 3 (4,4)
alt rows in all 62 (68,74) sts.

Shape shoulders
Cast off 3 (4,4) sts at beg of next 4 (8,4)
rows. Cast off 4 (0,5) sts at beg of next 4
(0,4) rows. Place rem 34 (36,39) sts onto
holder.

Front

Cast on and work as for Back until Front
meas 14 (16,18) cm from beg, ending
with wsr. Set chart on next row as
follows. (Work chart from right to left on
k rows, and left to right on p rows. Do not
weave contrast yarn, carry across back
of work, taking care to keep tension
even.)
1st row: k38 (42,46) MC, * k1 C, k1 MC,
rep from * 3 times, k1 C, MC to end.

2nd row: p30 (34,38) MC, * p1 C, p1 MC,
rep from * 4 times, p1 C, MC to end.
Cont chart as set from 3rd row, until work
meas 24 (26,28) cm from beg, ending
with wsr.

Shape armholes
Keeping chart correct, shape armholes as
for Back.
When chart is completed, work in MC
over all sts and cont until Front meas 35
(38,42) cm from beg, ending with wsr.

Shape neck

k27 (30,32) sts, turn. Working on these
sts only shape at neck edge of next and
foll alt rows by casting off 4 sts once, 3
sts once, 2 sts once, then dec 1 st until
14 (16,18) sts rem. Cont straight until
Front matches Back to shoulder, ending
at armhole edge.

Shape shoulder

Cast off 3 (4,4) sts at beg of next 2 (4,2)
alt rows.
Cast off 4 (0,5) sts at beg of next 2 (0,2)
rows.
Fasten off.

Neckband

Join right shoulder seam. With rsf, using
3.25 mm needles and MC, pick up and
k82 (88,92) sts evenly around neck edge,
including sts on holders.
Work in single rib until rib measures 3 cm
from beginning. Cast off loosely in rib.

To Make Up

Join left shoulder seam and neckband.

Armhole Bands

Using 3.25mm needles, MC and rsf, pick
up and k74 (82,90) sts evenly along
armhole edge. Rib as for neckband. Join
side and armband seams. Do not press.

There are many methods of casting
on. You should simply choose the
one which suits you best. Aim for a
neat edge with stitches that are not
too tight. If you find that your
casting on is too tight then it might
be best to use needles one size
larger for your casting on and then
change to the size specified in the
first row of the pattern. You should
use the same technique if your
casting off is too tight. It is
especially important to have a
loosely cast off edge when working
neckbands and cuffs to keep the
elasticity in the ribbing. When
casting off ribbing it gives a better
finish if knit stitches are knitted and
purl stitches purled before they are
cast off. This is known as casting
off "in rib".

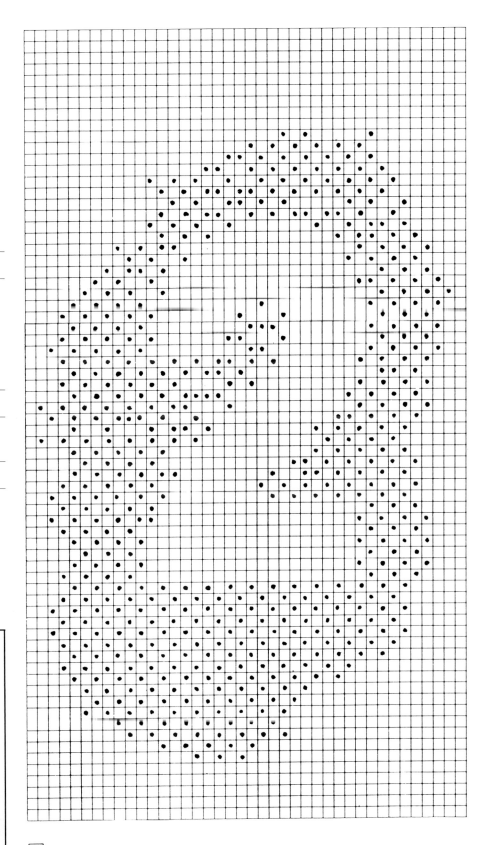

●   C

SPORTING HERO
Top

To fit ages 8yrs, 10yrs, 12yrs

Materials

Cleckheaton Country 8 ply 50 g balls
Main Colour (MC)   9 (10,11) balls
Contrast (C)   1 ball
One pair each 4mm and 3.25mm, and 1
set of 3.25mm needles, cable needle,
stitch holder.

Measurements

Garment measures	82	91	96	cm
Back length	46	51	56	cm
Sleeve seam	36	40	43	cm

TENSION
22 sts to 10cm over st st, using
4mm needles.
**IT IS IMPORTANT TO KNIT A
TENSION SQUARE AND TO
WORK TO STATED TENSION IN
ORDER TO OBTAIN REQUIRED
MEASUREMENTS. IF YOUR
SQUARE IS BIGGER USE FINER
NEEDLES. IF YOUR SQUARE IS
SMALLER USE THICKER
NEEDLES.**

SPECIAL ABBREVIATIONS

"C8B" = Slip next 4 sts onto a cable
needle and leave at back of work, k4,
then k4 from cable needle.
"C8F" = Slip next 4 sts onto a cable
needle and leave at front of work, k4,
then k4 from cable needle.

Back

Using 3.25mm needles and C, cast on 90
(98,106) sts.
***1st row:** k2, *p2, k2, rep from * to
end.
2nd row: p2, *k2, p2, rep from * to end.
Using MC, **3rd row:** knit.
4th row: as 2nd row.***
Rep 1st and 2nd rows until band meas 6
(6,7)cm from beg, ending with a 2nd row
and inc 10 (12,10) sts evenly across last
row. 100 (110,116) sts.
Change to 4mm needles and beg patt.

1st row: k19 (24,27), p2, k12, p2, k30,
p2, k12, p2, k19 (24,27).
2nd and alt rows: p19 (24,27), k2, p12,
k2, p30, k2, p12, k2, p19 (24,27).
3rd row: as 1st row.
5th row: k19 (24,27), p2, "C8B", k4, p2,
k30, p2, "C8B", k4, p2, k19 (24,27).
7th row: as 1st row.
9th row: as 1st row.
11th row: as 1st row.
13th row: k19 (24,27), p2, k4, "C8F", p2,
k30, p2, k4, "C8F", p2, k19 (24,27).
15th row: as 1st row.
16th row: as 2nd row.
Rows 1 to 16 inclusive form patt.
Cont in patt until work measures 28
(31,35)cm from beg, working last row on
wrong side.

Shape armholes
Keeping patt correct, cast off 5 (6,7) sts
at beg of next 2 rows.**
Dec one st at each end of next row and
foll alt rows until 80 (84,88) sts rem.
Work 43 (45,49) rows.

Shape shoulders
Cast off 8 (8,9) sts at beg of next 4 rows,
then 9 sts at beg of foll 2 rows.
Leave rem 30 (34,34) sts on a stitch
holder.

Front

Work as for back to **
Divide for 'V' neck.
Next row: k2tog, patt 43 (47,49), turn.
Keeping patt correct, dec one st at each
end of alt rows 4 (6,6) times, then dec
one st at neck edge only in alt rows 2
(1,0) times, then in foll 4th rows until 25
(25,27) sts rem.
Work 3 (5) rows.

Shape shoulder
Cast off 8 (8,9) sts at beg of next row and
foll alt row.
Work 1 row.
Cast off.
Join MC to rem sts at centre, patt to last
2 sts, k2tog. Complete other side of neck
and armhole to correspond, noting to
work 1 row more before shaping
shoulder.

Sleeves

Using 3.25mm needles and C, cast on 38
(38,42) sts.
Work from *** to *** of back.
Rep 1st and 2nd rows until band meas
6cm from beg, ending with a 2nd row and
inc 12 (16,16) sts evenly across last row.
50 (54,58) sts.
Change to 4mm needles and beg patt.

1st row: k1 (2,3), p2, k12, p2, k16
(18,20), p2, k12, p2, k1 (2,3).
2nd and alt rows: knit all knit sts and purl
all purl sts as they appear.
3rd row: inc in first st, k0 (1,2), p2, k12,
p2, k16 (18,20), p2, k12, p2, k0 (1,2), inc
in last st. 52 (56,60) sts.
5th row: k2 (3,4), p2, "C8B", k4, p2, k16
(18,20), p2, "C8B", k4, p2, k2 (3,4).
Keeping placement of cables correct as
for back, cont in patt as placed in last 5
rows, inc one st at each end of 2nd
(2nd,4th) and foll 4th (4th,6th) rows until
there are 62 (66,82) sts, then in foll 6th
(6th,8th) rows until there are 80 (88,90)
sts, noting to work extra sts in st st.
Cont in patt without shaping until side
edge meas 36 (40,43)cm from beg,
working last row on wrong side.

Shape top
Keeping patt correct, cast off 3 (3,4) sts
at beg of next 2 rows.
Dec one st at each end of next and foll alt
rows until 56 (60,56) sts rem, then in
every row until 14 sts rem.
Cast off.

Neckband

Using back stitch, join shoulder seams.
With right side facing using set of 3.25mm
needles and MC, beg at left shoulder
seam, knit up 56 (60,64) sts evenly along
left side of neck, knit up 2 sts from centre
(centre sts), knit up 56 (60,64) sts evenly
along right side of neck, then knit across
sts from back st holder. 144 (156,164) sts.
1st round: *k2, p2, rep from * to end.
2nd round: rib to within one st of centre 2
sts, k2 tog, sl 1, k1, psso, rib to end.
Rep 2nd round 3 (3,5) times.
Using C, **next round:** knit.
Next round: as 2nd round.
Cast off loosely in rib.

To Make Up

Using back stitch, join side and sleeve
seams. Sew in sleeves. Sew edges of
neckband in position, crossing right over
left.

A dropped stitch which has caused
a ladder is quite simple to deal with
providing you have a crochet hook
handy. Simply use the hook to knit
or purl each stitch up the ladder
until you reach the row on the
needle. It is very important to pick
up the stitches knitwise in the knit
rows and purlwise in the purl rows.

DREAM OF A BALLERINA
Ballet Set

To fit ages 4yrs, 6yrs, 8yrs, 10yrs

Materials

Panda Angoretta 50g balls 8 ply
Top   4 (5,5,6) balls
Leg Warmers   3 (3,4,4) balls
One pair each 4mm and 3.25mm needles,
1m ribbon.

Measurements

Garment measures	65	70	75	80 cm
Back length	31	33	35	38 cm
Sleeve seam	28	33	38	40 cm
Leg warmers	36	42	48	52 cm

TENSION
22 sts and 30 rows to 10cm over st
st using 4mm needles.
**IT IS IMPORTANT TO KNIT A
TENSION SQUARE AND TO
WORK TO STATED TENSION IN
ORDER TO OBTAIN REQUIRED
MEASUREMENTS. IF YOUR
SQUARE IS BIGGER USE FINER
NEEDLES. IF YOUR SQUARE IS
SMALLER USE THICKER
NEEDLES.**

TOP

Back

Using 3.25mm needles cast on 72
(78,84,90) sts.
Work in single rib (k1, p1) for 16 rows.
Change to 4mm needles. **
Work 78 (84,90,98) rows st st.

Shape shoulders
Cast off 11 (13,14,15) sts at beg of next
2 rows, then 11 (12,14,15) sts at beg of
next 2 rows.
Cast off rem 28 (28,28,30) sts.

Right Front

Work as for back to **
Next row: k.
2nd row: p to last 6 sts, p2tog tbl, k4.
3rd row: k4, sl 1, k1, psso, k to end.

Repeat 2nd and 3rd rows a further 7
(8,10,16) times. 56 (60,62, 56) sts. Work 1
row. Dec at shaped edge as before in next
3 rows.
Rep last 4 rows a further 4 (4,3,1) times.
41 (45,50,50) sts.
Dec at shaped edge in alt rows until 30
(33,37,43) sts rem.
Dec in foll 4th rows until 26 (29,32,34) sts
rem. Work 3 (5,5,5) rows.

Shape shoulders
Cast off 11 (13,14,15) sts at beg of next
row, then 11 (12,14,15) sts at beg of foll alt
row.

Neckband

Continue on rem 4 sts working in garter st
until band is long enough to fit across half
back neck. Cast off.

Left Front

Work to correspond with right front,
reversing shaping (thus working "p2tog" in
place of "p2tog tbl", and "k2tog" in place
of "sl 1, k1, psso").

Sleeves

Using 3.25mm needles cast on 38
(38,40,42) sts.
Work 16 rows rib as for Back.
Change to 4mm needles and st st, inc at
each end of 5th and foll 4th rows until
there are 66 (58,70,74) sts.
2nd, 3rd and 4th sizes only: inc in foll 6th
rows until there are (70,80,84) sts. Work
7 (7,7,9) rows. Cast off loosely.

To Make Up

Do not press. Join shoulder seams. Sew in
sleeves, placing centre of sleeves to
shoulder seams. Sew sleeve and side
seams, leaving an opening on right side
for ribbon. Sew ribbon to front bands.

LEG WARMERS
Using 4mm needles cast on 78 (82,86,90)
sts.
1st row: k2, *p2, k2, rep from * to end.
2nd row: p2, *k2, p2, rep from * to end.
Rep these 2 rows until work meas 36
(42,48,52) cm.
Cast off loosely in rib.

To Make Up

Do not press. Sew leg seams.

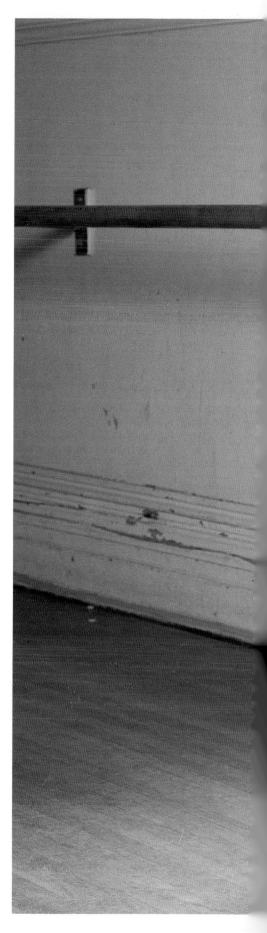